WATERSIDE
In Northam...

Judy Smith

COUNTRYSIDE BOOKS

NEWBURY, BERKSHIRE

First published 2000
© Judy Smith 2000

COUNTRYSIDE BOOKS
3 Catherine Road
Newbury, Berkshire

To view our complete range of books,
please visit us at
www.countrysidebooks.co.uk

ISBN 1 85306 611 7

Designed by Graham Whiteman
Maps by the author
Photographs by Reginald Hayes

Produced through MRM Associates Ltd., Reading
Typeset by Techniset Typesetters, Newton-le-Willows
Printed by Woolnough Bookbinding Ltd., Irthlingborough

Contents

Area Map Showing Location of the Walks

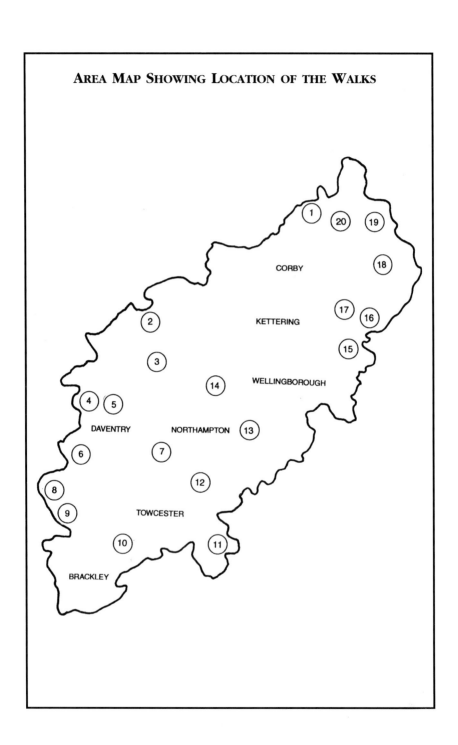

Walk

PUBLISHER'S NOTE

We hope that you obtain considerable enjoyment from this book; great care has been taken in its preparation. Although at the time of publication all routes followed public rights of way or permitted paths, diversion orders can be made and permissions withdrawn.

We cannot, of course, be held responsible for such diversion orders and any inaccuracies in the text which result from these or any other changes to the routes nor any damage which might result from walkers trespassing on private property. We are anxious though that all details covering the walks are kept up to date and would therefore welcome information from readers which would be relevant to future editions.

INTRODUCTION

Having for many years enjoyed the inland waterways from our family narrow boat, I was very pleased to be given the opportunity to write this book and share some of my enthusiasm! Northamptonshire is well blessed with waterways – canals, rivers, reservoirs and lakes are here in plenty, with many good footpaths running beside them. Exploring them again for this book has been the greatest pleasure.

Through the heart of the county runs the Grand Union Canal and, of course, there is a good towpath beside it. It is an exciting, lively canal, always busy with holidaymakers, but with so many reminders of a bygone age. The canal enters Northamptonshire dramatically on a high aqueduct over the River Ouse at Cosgrove, an aqueduct which caused much trouble in its construction. Further on, the tunnel at Blisworth was a source of even more problems and eventually boats were taken through by 'legging' – walking on the walls! At Nether Heyford there are remains of old wharves where cargoes were unloaded, and at Weedon, a high embankment whose breach once caused the flooding of Northampton. At Norton Junction, the old toll house was for many years the base of the Salvation Army's mission to the boat people. Braunston was a centre of commercial trade on the waterways, the hub and the pulse of the canal system. Boat people lived on here for years after all trading ceased and their story and the story of the canals is well told in the Canal Museum at Stoke Bruerne.

Two other canals have a place in this book, the North Oxford and the Leicester Branch of the Grand Union. Both are quieter, more tranquil canals than the Grand Union mainline and on both you can enjoy the natural banks with a wealth of flowers in summertime.

Canals need reservoirs to feed their summit levels, and tiny Boddington in the far west provides an attractive round walk. At the other end of the scale, 700 acre Pitsford, supplying water for Northampton town, offers a pleasant and easy path around its shores and the smaller, tree-fringed Hollowell should not be missed.

The rivers of Northamptonshire are surprisingly many! Everyone knows the Nene, the seventh longest river in Britain, arising in the west and crossing the county on its way to the Wash. Its valley is wide, green and fertile and here are some of the loveliest villages and churches in England. The valley has been extensively quarried for gravel, leaving us with many lakes and nature reserves where it is possible to enjoy wildfowl, butterflies and dragonflies.

But in Northamptonshire there are six other rivers, all of them arising within the county. And what is more, no river enters the county from outside. Surely Northamptonshire must be the highest place in England! At least, this was the logic applied by the ancients, who deemed Arbury Hill, all of 225 metres, to be England's highest peak. The area of the Northamptonshire Heights around Arbury Hill is so pretty that I have taken the liberty of including the long classic walk known as the 'Three River Ramble' – it crosses in turn the Cherwell, the Leam and the Nene, each of which arises on the slopes of Arbury Hill. Other infant rivers form the county boundaries, and walks have been included beside the Welland in the north and the Great Ouse in the south, both pretty rural rambles.

My own favourite has been saved till last – the walk around Blatherwycke Lake from King's Cliffe. The remoteness of the valley of Willow Brook is heightened by the finding of a lonely statue in a cornfield, a reminder of times long gone. The deep forest on the way home and the old grey stone houses of King's Cliffe give a feeling of timelessness difficult to describe.

Yet another pleasurable experience has been visiting the pubs en route! There are so many that can be described as 'different' – pubs in tiny villages with extensive menus of exotic fare; pubs with relics of the past on the walls, Civil War armour or antique carpenters' tools; a lounge bar furnished at the turn of the 20th century; a 'beer garden' on a village green with peacocks. All these and more are there for you to find, and if after all this, you still have time to spare, there are suggestions for places of interest to visit nearby.

Northamptonshire is well waymarked, and the routes of all these walks should be quite easy to follow. A sketch map has been given for each, but you would do well to take along with you the recommended Landranger map – or, even better, one of the larger scale Explorer maps which are now being produced.

In conclusion, I must thank my husband, Eric, who has tramped many watery ways at my side and my father, Reginald Hayes, who has taken all the photographs. Writing this book has taken up much of my time and I have appreciated their help and support.

I wish you many happy hours of pleasant walking beside the waterways of Northamptonshire.

Judy Smith

HARRINGWORTH AND THE RIVER WELLAND

The winding River Welland forms the north-western border of the county, gaining strength here on its journey to The Wash. Beside the pretty village of Harringworth, its wide valley is spanned by a huge viaduct – a monumental feat of engineering! Walking beside and above the winding river brings you to the attractive Rutland village of Barrowden and its Northamptonshire twin, Wakerley.

The medieval bridge at Wakerley

Arising from countless springs in the village of Sibbertoft, the Welland almost immediately assumes its role as guardian of the county boundary. For some 30 miles it separates Northamptonshire from Lincolnshire and Rutland before leaving to cross the fens on its way to the sea. Here the river flows through a scooped-out valley of rich green farmland with sparse but most delightful villages.

Harringworth seems the epitome of rural England, a place where warm golden-stone, thatched houses, a medieval church and an old coaching inn are grouped around the ancient market cross. And across this pastoral scene strides a huge dark-blue monster on many legs, the much famed Victorian viaduct, whose huge arches completely dwarf the tiny cottages beneath. Three miles down river from Harringworth is another village which, though different, rivals it for beauty. At Barrowden, the stone houses, inn and church are clustered this time around chestnut-shaded greens, and here a village duckpond is added to the picture. Leaving this delightful spot, an old packhorse bridge takes you over the Welland to the smaller but interesting village of Wakerley, once more in Northamptonshire. On the return, the views across the valley are excellent, and even that viaduct seems attractive from a distance. A seat is placed on the hill as you descend into Harringworth where you may take a final, long, overall view before reaching the village.

Back in Harringworth, the White Swan certainly merits a visit. Just how old it is, is a difficult question. The staircase is Jacobean, and the fireplace Tudor, but there are features from every century here. In fact, there is so much of interest around the place that you could almost be diverted from your prime purpose! But when your gaze falls upon the menu board you will soon be recalled, and the choices are outstanding. Try their own Chicken Harringworth, where the mushroom-stuffed chicken breast is served grilled with Stilton or, for a vegetarian dish, baked courgettes with mixed nut stuffing. An excellent range of beers and cask ales are on offer as well as an interesting selection of wines.

Telephone: 01572 747543.

- **HOW TO GET THERE:** From the A43 Corby-Stamford road, turn left where signposted at Bulwick to reach Harringworth (3 miles).
- **PARKING:** On quiet roadsides in the village or at the White Swan for patrons.
- **LENGTH OF THE WALK:** 6 miles (shorter 2 mile option available). Map: OS Landranger 141 Kettering and Corby (GR 916973).

THE WALK

1. Before leaving the Market Cross (the White Swan is just a few yards away), glance around to see the very curious 'Gothic Chimney' on The Old Smithy. It is not in its original site, but is thought to have once been part of the old Manor House. Walk along the road in the

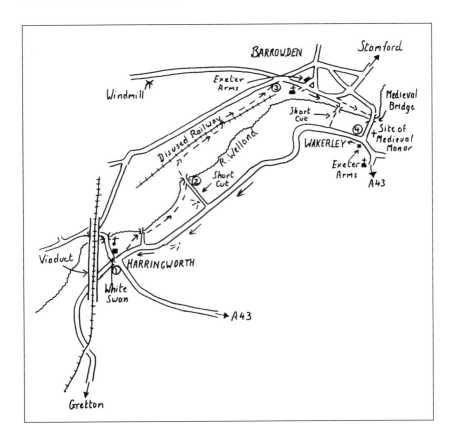

direction of Wakerley, where opposite Limes Farm a wooden fingerpost points across a field on the left. From here to Barrowden the route is along the Jurassic Way, and as such is very well waymarked. Crossing the field diagonally towards a rusty metal river bridge, a stile is seen in the hedge about 20 yards from the river bank. After crossing this, the path stays beside the much-winding river for about a mile. Ahead of you, the spire of Barrowden can be seen, and behind, the village of Harringworth and the viaduct in all its glory! The windmill at Morcott is on the hill on your left. The viaduct was built in just two years, between the summers of 1876 and 1878. In those two years were laid 20 million bricks, not to mention the stone and concrete foundations. All-in-all, the viaduct has 82 arches and carries the railway 3/4 mile across the valley. It is still in use today, although only freight trains cross it now.

2. The riverside path meets a broad track which crosses Turtle Bridge on the left. If you wish to make an early return to Harringworth, turn right here and follow this byway to the road. There are fine views of the valley as you climb. At the road, turn right to return to the village.

To continue with the main walk, cross the bridge – a sign proclaims you are now in Rutland – and climb towards the railway bridge. Before reaching it, a sign directs you into a field on the right. Beside the gate you will make your first encounter with a 'yellow-top pole' – Rutland's excellent route markers. Following signs and poles, you cross three fields, and in the fourth are directed to cross the railway track and turn right beside the hedge on the far side. You are now walking along the edge of a vast field, but about halfway along it, more poles appear directing you to bear diagonally left across two fields before cutting across the corner of a paddock and reaching the road. As you go, Wakerley church spire can be seen on the horizon on the right, and in front of it, the brick lime kilns which were built by prisoners of war and never used.

3. At the road turn right, and at the crossroads, right again. This brings you into Barrowden with the duckpond on your right and the most attractively-sited Exeter Arms on your left. It would be difficult to resist a pause here! When ready – keep ahead on the road through the village to reach a triangular green with bus-shelter. Bear right past this, and now you have a choice again. You can follow the Jurassic Way signs down the narrow track and cross the river and then a field to come out on the road at the edge of Wakerley. But if you wish to see the medieval bridge – and indeed yet another Exeter Arms – bear left here and continue into the field. A stile on the right leads you into a big field where you bear left around the jutting-out corner of the hedge. The bridge comes into view and the obligatory yellow pole beside it marks the stile you seek to reach the road. Turn right and cross the river, passing some rather strange houses which were once part of the station buildings here. Farther up the road, behind the hedge on the left, the humps and hollows in the field can explain the prevalence of 'Exeter Arms' around here! The Cecil family, who took the title 'Earl of Exeter,' once had a manor house on this site. It was abandoned by them after a series of misfortunes some 300 years ago – the family now live at Burghley House near Stamford. On reaching the T-junction by the Exeter Arms, turn right to walk down the long village street. Those who

The White Swan, Harringworth

have taken the short cut from Barrowden will join you near its end.

4. Continue on this quiet road all the way back to Harringworth – a distance of some 2½ miles. You will pass the field with the lime kilns and then climb to get some panoramic views of the valley. Near the top of the hill the viaduct comes into view and the wide landscape and richness of the hedgerows make this a most enjoyable walk home.

PLACES OF INTEREST NEARBY
More of the Great Outdoors can be enjoyed at nearby *Wakerley Great Wood* with its nature trails and permanent orienteering courses. Five miles north of Harringworth (take the Morcott road) is *Rutland Water* where you can enjoy fine views of the lake or take a walk around its perimeter path – a distance of 18 miles. But perhaps you should save that for another time!

WELFORD AND THE LEICESTER BRANCH OF THE GRAND UNION CANAL

Quieter than its parent main line, the Leicester Branch of the Grand Union winds its reed-fringed way below gently sloping hills. Moorhens and water-voles inhabit its lonely banks and you may be lucky enough to spot a kingfisher.

The wharf at Welford

The Leicester Branch of the Grand Union Canal is a far cry from the lively bustling main line to the south. Few pleasure craft turn north at Norton Junction – perhaps the cities of Leicester and Loughborough hold little attraction for the boating fraternity. And so the canal lies undisturbed and still, a peaceful place since the last commercial traffic passed some 50 years ago.

As with many canals, this one has a complex history. The canal serving the industrial cities of the North-East came south only as far as Market Harborough. The Grand Junction (later Grand Union) Canal from London to Birmingham ran well south of this and it was only in 1814 – quite late in the canal era – that the connection between the two was made. The route was planned and surveyed by one James Barnes, the more famous Thomas Telford's plans having been rejected as too expensive! Even Barnes' version needed two tunnels and two staircases of locks to cope with the changing elevations. But here the canal follows a winding course along the contour lines. On one side the wooded hills rise gently, while on the other the land falls away to give glimpses of Stanford Reservoir and the infant River Avon. Wildlife thrives in the reeds at the water's edge, herons and even kingfishers may be seen, and, in summer, the banks offer you a heady concoction of wild flowers. When at last you leave this tranquillity, there is a fine walk across the Hemplow Hills and good views before you return to your starting point.

Welford itself is a fascinating place with a colourful history. Once an important staging post on the Irish Mail Run, seven inns flourished in its main street. Of these, three only remain. The Shoulder of Mutton was established here in the 17th century, well before the advent of the mail coaches, and has prospered to this day. Inside, the atmosphere is friendly, the ceilings are low and beamed and the walls hung with horse-brasses and old photographs. This is a freehouse serving a good range of beers and ales. In the 'snacks' line, the toasted sandwiches are justly very popular, but you could upgrade to steak or a seafood platter should you be feeling more adventurous. The inn has a reputation with boaters holidaying on the canal, and welcomes children with such meals as Lock-keepers Delight and Narrowboat Special – splendid pseudonyms for fish fingers or sausage and chips! There is a small outdoor garden for fine days. Telephone: 01858 575375.

- **HOW TO GET THERE:** Welford stands on the A5199, 2 miles north of its junction with the A14. The Shoulder of Mutton is in the High Street.
- **PARKING:** Walkers may leave their cars in the Shoulder of Mutton car park. Otherwise there is easy parking in the quiet streets of Welford, perhaps close to the church.
- **LENGTH OF THE WALK:** 6$\frac{1}{2}$ miles. Map: OS Landranger 140 Leicester and Coventry (GR 643804).

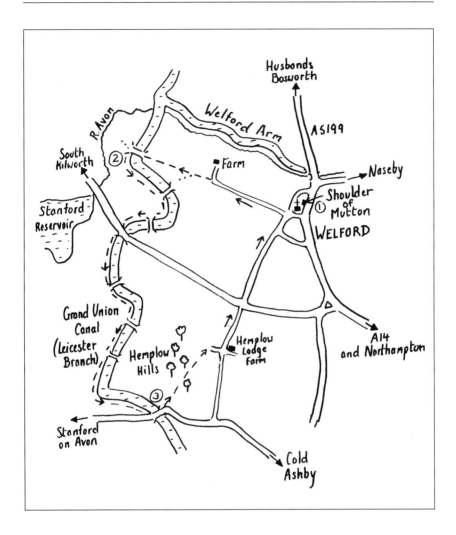

THE WALK

1. Leaving the Shoulder of Mutton, walk uphill beside the main road, and then turn right down Church Lane. At its end on the right is the very lovely and interesting church of St Mary (certainly worth a visit on your return), but now you should turn left along West End, and then take the first track on the right where a finger-post directs you to North Kilworth Mill. Where the next finger-post to the Mill points across fields on the left, keep straight ahead on the concrete track. Soon the track climbs uphill and there are good

15

views of Welford behind you. When the track swings sharply right to the farm, keep straight on, on the waymarked path ahead. The path climbs over the hill and there are excellent views. Ahead and to the left is Stanford Reservoir, through which flows the infant River Avon, here the boundary with Leicestershire. The two church spires ahead are those of North and South Kilworth, while far away to the right rises the spire of Husbands Bosworth, all three in foreign Leicestershire. Below you to the south the canal wends its lonely way around the foot of the hills.

The path is well waymarked and you should keep straight ahead (ignoring the path to the left). Soon the land begins to fall away, and you descend with the hedge on your right to reach the canal where you turn left to join the towpath.

2. Now you have a long stretch beside this most attractive of canals. It twists and turns, giving you many different views of Stanford Reservoir on the right. There are attractive red brick bridges, and soon you see ahead the wooded crowns of the Hemplow Hills. The canal itself enters a long pleasant area of woodland where the steep ivy-clad banks are home to the water-vole and others. At Bridge 31 you must tear yourself away from the scene.

3. Here you cross the canal bridge and take the footpath across the field on your left, now the route of the Jurassic Way. The path rises sharply to enter the woodland. Climbing quite steeply for a short distance, you reach the highest point of the Hemplow Hills. The view is hidden for a while as you take the winding path through the trees, but emerging on the field, a wide vista is revealed, and the canal is seen snaking away far below you to the left, and beyond it, the distant reservoir and river. Reaching the farm barns, you take the obvious track to the right, and then, at the track junction, bear left following the Jurassic Way signs. A long straight road brings you to a crossroads, where you go straight ahead to Welford and the welcoming Shoulder of Mutton.

PLACES OF INTEREST NEARBY

If you are interested in canals, *Welford wharf,* at the bottom end of the village on the Leicester road, is well worth a visit. It is the terminus of the Welford Arm, and in summertime sees the arrival and departure of a succession of brightly-painted narrow boats.

GUILSBOROUGH AND HOLLOWELL RESERVOIR

Hollowell is surely the most attractive of reservoirs, tucked away in its hidden valley. Sailing boats and myriads of wildfowl add to the watery scene, which on this walk is complemented by the fine old buildings and interesting inn at Guilsborough.

Hollowell Reservoir

North of Northampton, the land is gently rolling, patches of woodland being scattered between the red-earthy fields and green grazing land. Streams drain from the high ground to the west, and these have been used here to create two small reservoirs holding water for the surrounding area. In this countryside the reservoirs have an attractive setting while the nearby villages are likewise pleasant, with buildings of deep brownish-red local stone.

Close to the old village of Guilsborough, Hollowell Reservoir provides you with a splendid walk around its shores. It is managed by Anglian Water, who also supply fishing and bird watching permits here. And well they might, as the waters are thronged with wildfowl of all kinds! Ducks, geese and moorhens abound, while herons, grebes and cormorants are obvious competitors for the fishing rights. At weekends, the boats of the sailing club share the waters and enliven the scene again. The path around the shores is very pleasant, first winding through the shelter of Scots pines and mixed woodland before emerging to the breezy heights of the dam. The eastern shore is mostly open pasture.

The walk can be started from the reservoir car park, but Guilsborough itself is well worth a visit. There are many lovely old buildings but most striking of all is the Old Grammar School, a huge edifice of deep orange stone dating from 1668. Once used to provide the free education of 50 youths from the area, it is now converted to private dwellings, but the original character is well preserved.

Immediately opposite the Old Grammar School is the white-washed and thatched Ward Arms. The inn is just as pleasing inside as out, with low-beamed ceilings and high-backed wooden settles. You are everywhere reminded of Guilsborough's associations with the Battle of Naseby - General Fairfax and his troops camped on the hill here before setting out for that historic conflict. Pictures of Parliamentarians and Royalists, armour, swords and weapons adorn every wall, providing a history lesson to be imbibed along with your meal! A range of real ales and draught cider is on offer, along with a good varied menu. Grills are popular, as is home-made steak-and-ale pie.

Telephone: 01604 740265.

- **HOW TO GET THERE:** From the A5199 Northampton-Leicester road, turn west where signposted to Guilsborough, 3 miles south of the A14 junction. The reservoir car park is just a few hundred yards on along this minor road, while Guilsborough is almost a mile further.
- **PARKING:** There is a small car park at the north end of the reservoir. In Guilsborough there is parking on quiet roadsides and also at the Ward Arms for patrons.
- **LENGTH OF THE WALK:** Around the perimeter of the reservoir, 3 miles. Starting from Guilsborough, the total distance will be 5 miles. Map: OS Landranger 141 Kettering and Corby (GR 677729 – The Ward Arms).

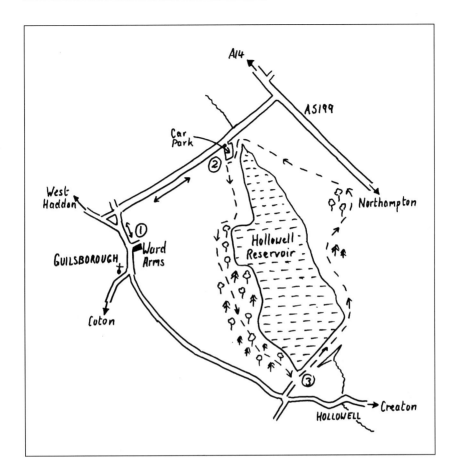

THE WALK

1. Leaving the Ward Arms, walk uphill to the top of the village. On reaching the village green (with a most curious lock-up at its centre), turn right down Nortoft, and continue downhill and along the road to reach the reservoir car park on the right. The reservoir hides from your sight until the very last moment!

2. Walk through the car park and keep ahead on the path beside the hedge. Soon a stile (thoughtfully accompanied by a dog gate, as are all the stiles around the reservoir) will lead you into the woodland. Scots pines are prevalent, their tall bare trunks affording views of the water beyond. But there are deciduous trees also,

19

giving fine colours in the autumn. After another stile, the path bears right along the peripheral hedge, but soon swings back to the water again. A long green avenue between the tall pines is followed by a stile, after which the now stony path keeps ahead to reach the garden of a house. Bearing left here, you will see the gates of the sailing club on the left.

3. Just before reaching the tarmac road, turn sharp left over the stile to cross the dam. Suddenly you are exposed to the elements and the wind whips little waves to break against the wall below. Nevertheless it is a popular spot for fishermen! Turning left at the far end, you have the sheep for company and can follow the shores to bring you back to the car park. But there is also a path higher up beside the perimeter hedge, which at one point passes through another patch of woodland and always provides you with good views. Across the water the spire of St Ethelreda's church at Guilsborough peeps through the trees, while Nortoft Hill, ahead and to the left, was the hill on which General Fairfax and his men spent the night before Naseby. At the top end of the reservoir, the path crosses a little bridge before again reaching the car park, from which you can retrace your steps to Guilsborough.

PLACES OF INTEREST NEARBY

One mile south of Guilsborough, just before Ravensthorpe Reservoir, is *Coton Manor* with its renowned gardens. Carefully and personally tended, these landscaped gardens with bluebell wood and wild flower meadow, are overlooked by a lovely 17th-century manor house. Home-made lunches and teas are served. Open summer afternoons (except Mondays and Tuesdays). Telephone: 01604 740219.

There are more fine gardens 3 miles to the east at Cottesbrooke. These surround *Cottesbrooke Hall*, an elegant Queen Anne mansion, said to be the model for Jane Austen's *Mansfield Park*. The Hall is famed for its collection of sporting paintings (Stubbs and Ben Marshall), fine 18th-century furniture and porcelain. Here, too, you can enjoy a home-made tea! The Hall and gardens are open on Thursday afternoons, the gardens alone at other times also. Telephone: 01604 505808.

WALK 4

BESIDE THE NORTH OXFORD CANAL AT BRAUNSTON

Braunston is something of a mecca for inland waterways enthusiasts! From the village, this walk climbs Barby Hill with views across Warwickshire and returns along the peaceful North Oxford Canal, guided by the spire of Braunston church.

Entrance to the marina at Braunston

Do you always keep the tastiest morsel on your plate to be eaten last? If you do, then this walk should suit you well! The whole trip is delightful, but the walk home along the North Oxford Canal is a real treat. Here in summertime, wild flowers in profusion grace the natural banks, while saplings of ash and willow bend their heads to touch the water. Ducks and moorhens shuffle in and out of reed beds beside ancient 'ridge and furrow' fields where cattle now graze. At the end of this stretch is the excitement of Braunston junction with its attractive twin iron bridges, followed by a lively towpath scene where painted canalware is peddled from brightly coloured barges amid a flurry of narrow boat arrivals and departures.

The walk begins with a long path across country between Braunston and Barby. This countryside is the 'Feldon' – the land south of the Avon, as opposed to the 'Arden' in the north. The Arden was wooded, but the Feldon with its fewer trees and clay soil was intensely farmed. So it is today, although the farming in these parts seems to be largely sheep and cattle.

Braunston village is separated from Braunston canalside by a tarmacked track across the fields. On the High Street, there is a fine old 17th-century pub, oozing with character, the Old Plough. Here you can enjoy a well-served standard range of fare with one or two home-cooked specials such as beef bourguinnone and shepherd's pie. The desserts are interesting – whisky-flavoured mousse is certainly original, as is something called 'Eye of the Storm'! A good range of real ales is on offer as is a huge selection of malts! Look out for the autographed photos of celebrities on the wall!

Telephone: 01788 890000.

- **HOW TO GET THERE:** Braunston lies just off the A45 road, 3 miles north-west of Daventry.
- **PARKING:** There is parking at Braunston Marina which lies off the A45 just before the turn into the village. The Old Plough is in Braunston High Street, and there is parking for patrons in the car park behind the pub.
- **LENGTH OF THE WALK:** 6^1/$_2$ miles. Maps: The walk unfortunately spans 3 maps – OS Landrangers 152 Northampton and Milton Keynes, 140 Leicester and Coventry, and 151 Stratford-upon-Avon (GR 540658, Braunston Marina).

THE WALK

1. From the car parking area beside the marina, head for the canal side and double back over the attractive iron bridge which spans the entrance to the marina. Cross the canal on the brick bridge, and take the tarmacked footpath uphill to reach Braunston High Street. The Old Plough is diagonally across the road to the left. Cross the road diagonally to the right to a narrow one-way road which will take you through to Church Street. Turn left on Church Street and opposite the Old Plough car park (you may have parked here) a sign directs you to the public footpath to Barby. Following this, you

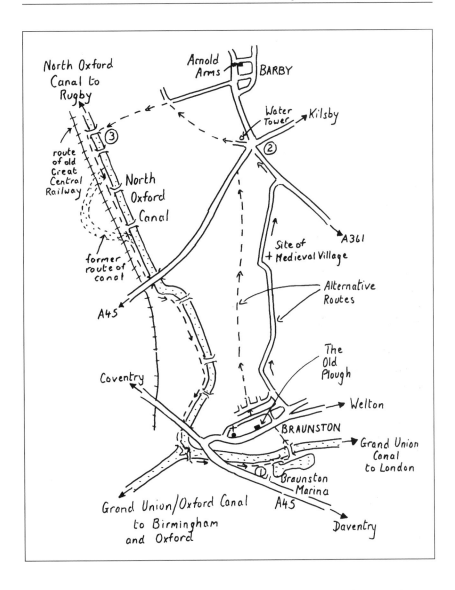

come to yet another road of newish houses. Now you have a choice! At the bottom of the close ahead (Countryside), a waymarked gate takes you into a field. The route across the fields to Barby is very well waymarked all the way, with good stiles, gates and bridges. There is only one possible snag – this is cow country! Just about every field you will pass through is home to grazing cattle, which although not normally a problem, could cause difficulties if you have a dog with you. The alternative is a walk up a very quiet and pleasant road which reaches the same point in about 2 miles.

If you decide to take the field path, there should be no difficulty following the route across the fields. On finally reaching the road, turn right for about 300 yards to arrive at the crossroads with the water tower. If you have decided not to tackle the cows, turn right along the road of new houses and continue to its end to meet Barby Lane. Here turn left and continue on the road. After the sharp left hand bend, the humps and hollows of a deserted village can be seen in the fields on the right. Further on there are fine views across the Warwickshire Plain, and you may be able to pick out the canal below you. At the road junction, turn left for about 500 yards to arrive at the crossroads with the water tower.

2. Continuing from the crossroads, a wooden footpath sign directs you up a track to the left of the water tower. There are now wide views to the north, where the masts of Rugby radio station can be seen. Where the track swings left, continue over the stile ahead (waymarked) and along beside the field. Another 'stile' with a white-painted top leads you into a second field and continuing beside the hedge on the left you reach a wide field gate. Through this, a rough grassy lane leads you on to a track junction. Now follow the footpath sign pointing ahead and to the left which takes you into another field in which you keep beside the left hand hedge. You are now coming off the top of Barby Hill, and facing west towards Warwickshire – your canal walk will take you briefly into that county. The trig. height in the field on your left declares an elevation of 161 metres.

At its end, the field has a small projection, at the far hedge of which is a stile. After this, the route crosses the edge of another field and then descends along the right-hand hedge of the next two fields. Soon you can see the canal ahead, and the bridge you will cross over to reach it. The rather foreboding fenced buildings to the right are those of the Young Offenders Institution at Onley.

3. Over the bridge, turn left on to the grassy canal towpath. Between Bridges 83 and 84 the canal is in a narrow cutting lined on both sides by ash trees. The original route of the canal was here behind the trees on a wide loop to the right. After Bridge 84 you

Braunston church seen across the 'ridge and furrow' fields

can see the track-bed of the former Great Central Railway, where the last train passed in 1966. The old concrete signal stands sadly against the skyline! Continuing ahead, the canal twists and turns again, and soon you are facing the lovely spire of Braunston church on its hill, with the stump of a windmill beside. Sheep and cattle graze the 'ridge and furrow' fields of the opposite bank. Passing moored narrow boats, you reach the junction with the Grand Union and its fine black and white Horsley Iron Works bridges. Braunston was a one-time centre of canal trading and many of the great carrying companies had a base here. Now the commerce is all gone, and with it the families who spent their hard-working lives on the boats. Before you return to your car, take a moment to read the plaque on the iron bridge over the marina entrance.

PLACES OF INTEREST NEARBY
For something different, and a glimpse of genuine old Northamptonshire, visit the village of *Ashby St Ledgers*, 3 miles away to the north-east. Here is a lovely old manor house with a 14th-century church beside it. In the gatehouse of the manor, which still stands, the Gunpowder Plot was hatched – and, refreshingly, there is no plaque to tell you so!

WELTON AND NORTON JUNCTION ON THE GRAND UNION

The quiet Leicester Branch of the Grand Union meets with its livelier mainline at pretty Norton Junction, where the old toll-house still stands to remind us of trading days. Travelling west, there are fine views across open country before the canal is slowly engulfed by a wooded cutting at the approach to Braunston Tunnel.

The old toll-house at Norton Junction

Between the locks at Long Buckby and those at Braunston the Grand Union Canal runs an attractive course. This section is known as Braunston Summit, and at first the canal is raised on an embankment, giving wide views across the sheep-dotted countryside to the north. On the south side, the narrow towpath is tree-shaded, at times wandering between the clumps of ash and willow dipping to the water, and the banks are rich with summer flowers. Farther west, the land rises and the embankment gives way to a green shady cutting before the canal is swallowed up into Braunston Tunnel.

Before reaching this lovely stretch of the Grand Union, the walk leads you briefly beside that most peaceful and remote of canals, the Leicester Branch. In the 35 miles to Leicester, its peace is shaken but briefly as it passes beside the M1 and railway through the Watford Gap, north-east of Welton. Joining the canal on this walk, the drone of the M1 can still be heard in the distance, but as you continue along the grassy towpath through the woodland, peace is restored in time for you to enjoy Norton Junction, where you meet the mainline of the Grand Union. This attractive junction is a lively and colourful place in summertime with moored boats as well as the many arrivals and departures. Buckby Top Lock is just a few yards away and the New Inn beside it has canalside tables from which you can view the scene before continuing. Welton village itself is well worthy of exploration on your return. Sheltering on a hillside, there are some fine old stone houses to appreciate, but you are bound to notice the wealth of splendid trees. To the west of the village once stood a grand house known as Welton Place. The owners of the house were the Clarke family, great gardeners who created in its grounds a landscape of cedars around an ornamental, lily-strewn lake. The garden flower clarkia bears their name. The new houses of Clarke's Way are now built on the site which overlooks the preserved lake and trees.

Further along the road is the old brown-stone church and, just after it, the thatched and whitewashed White Horse presents an attractive sight. This is an inn which feels homely inside, with beams, white-washed walls and low ceilings. There is a pleasant restaurant area. The menu is fairly standard, but it is very well served and certainly the ploughman's is personally recommended! A good selection of beers and ales is on offer.

Telephone: 01327 702820.

- **HOW TO GET THERE:** Welton can be reached by turning where signed off the A5 at Watford.
- **PARKING:** On quiet roadsides in the village. There is a very small parking area at the White Horse for patrons.
- **LENGTH OF THE WALK:** 4½ miles. Map: OS Landranger 152 Northampton and Milton Keynes (GR 582661).

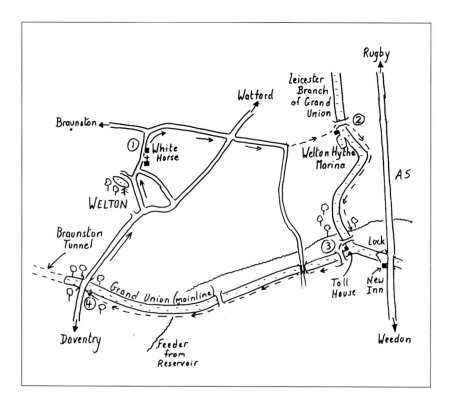

THE WALK

1. Leaving the White Horse, walk uphill away from the church. At the junction, turn right (Watford). From this road there are wide views all around, and the spire at Daventry can be seen on its hill to your right. At the crossroads, cross straight over. Where the road swings right, continue ahead on a bridleway which follows the hedgeline along, around and down to the buildings at Welton Hythe Marina. A waymark here directs you to skirt the back of these buildings and soon you cross the canal bridge.

2. Turn right (i.e. do not go under the bridge) along the towpath, passing the marina on the opposite side. This is now a most pleasant stretch of canal. The towpath is wide and grassy and woodland comes down to the opposite bank. Very soon you reach Norton Junction, and the Grand Union itself. Looking to the left, Buckby Top Lock can be seen, with the New Inn beside it.

Back at the junction, cross the white footbridge (it has replaced a difficult swingbridge – you will see the old arc rails on the far side). The path goes on behind the old toll-house which was until the 1950s the home base of the Fieldings, a Salvation Army couple who ran their own mission boats and worked among the boat people for many years. *Minnow*, the tiny punt now proudly restored and displayed beside the junction, belonged to them.

3. Continue over the brick bridge and turn right on to the towpath alongside the Grand Union. The narrow track winds up and down through waterside trees and would scarcely be much use in the days of horse-drawn barges, but makes a pleasant enough walk now. Across the canal the green fields sweep up to Welton village, a cluster of brown stone houses and a stubby church on the wooded hillside. The canal passes under two more attractive brick bridges, each retaining its rubbing bars, the iron strips grooved by the towropes of yesteryear. This is a summit – albeit only 357 feet – and as such has need of water as every boat passing on this busy route will take away with it a lockful. The large Daventry Reservoir, whose dam is seen over the fields on the left, provides its main supply by means of a feeder which enters in the stretch after Bridge 7. At the next bridge, no 8, you leave the canal, but before doing so, you might like to go under the bridge and look along the deep tree-lined cutting to the eerie mouth of Braunston Tunnel.

4. Climb up the path to the road just before the bridge. Turn right along the pavement and follow it for just over $1/2$ mile to Welton. Pass the red brick gates of Welton Manor where yews and chestnuts overhang the wall and shortly cross the road and turn left up Churchill Road. As the road climbs, you can see on the left the fine cedars of former Welton Place. Passing Clarke's Way, you may be tempted to divert to gain a glimpse of the lake between the houses. Continuing ahead, Kiln Lane is passed, and then the church, with its sad gravestone of a child beside the wall. A mere few paces ahead of you the White Horse awaits.

PLACES OF INTEREST NEARBY
If, after all this, you find yourself becoming a canal enthusiast, *Braunston* is just a tunnel length away – or about $2^1/2$ miles by road. It is one of the great centres of the inland waterways.

BADBY AND THE
THREE RIVER RAMBLE

Three rivers, the Cherwell, the Leam and the Nene, arise on the slopes of Arbury Hill. Meeting the source of each of the three rivers in turn, this is a long walk through the rolling patchwork landscape of the Northamptonshire Heights, but it really is too good to be missed!

The medieval packhorse bridge at Charwelton

Rising to all of 225 metres, Arbury Hill was once thought by locals to be the highest peak in England! The logic behind this assumption was that here was a hill in the centre of the country from whose slopes rivers ran in all directions. That certainly is true – the Nene flows east to the Wash, the Cherwell south to join the Thames, and the Leam north-west to meet the Avon – but pretty Arbury Hill scarcely fits the bill as England's greatest mountain! The Three River Ramble was originally designed as a walk from the county's only Youth Hostel at Badby. The route describes a huge circle around

Arbury Hill and its slightly lesser companion, Sharman's Hill and so crosses, in turn, each of the infant rivers. The countryside here is delightful, gently undulating and with ever-changing views. Badby, at the start of the walk has been described as the prettiest village in Northamptonshire and its woods are well-known for their bluebell display in spring. Other delights on this walk are the landscaped parkland at Fawsley, the ancient church in the sheep-field at Church Charwelton and the 15th century packhorse bridge at Charwelton itself.

The pubs here must surely be the pride of Northamptonshire! You will not have gone very far when you meet the Fox and Hounds at Charwelton with its varied restaurant menu. At Helidon, that attractive old stone pub the Red Lion serves excellent and imaginative snacks and meals every lunchtime and evening. At Staverton, the menu has to be seen to be believed! Salmon with raspberries in champagne, wild boar with forrestiere sauce or kangaroo with maple and gooseberries may not be the most suitable mid-walk snack – but you could always return.

If you can resist them all and return to Badby with appetite intact, The Windmill awaits you. Here is the most English of pubs – a white cottage with thatched roof and colourful hanging baskets opposite a village green. The menu is excellent – venison burgers with creamy pepper sauce, roast barbary duck breast, and plenty more. But there are also interesting 'snacks' such as triple-decker sandwiches which it is a real pleasure to eat outside, accompanied by one of the many beers and ales. The setting here seems a fitting conclusion to what is possibly Northamptonshire's best walk!

Telephone: 01327 702363.

- **HOW TO GET THERE:** Badby lies just east of the A361, 2 miles south of Daventry.
- **PARKING:** On quiet roadsides in the village. There may be parking behind the Windmill for patrons.
- **LENGTH OF THE WALK:** 11 miles (a long walk – but well worth the effort!). Maps: OS Landrangers 152 Northampton and Milton Keynes, and 151 Stratford-on-Avon (GR 559589).

THE WALK

1. From the Windmill, walk uphill, away from the green. Turn left up Vicarage Hill to where the lovely 14th-century church overlooks

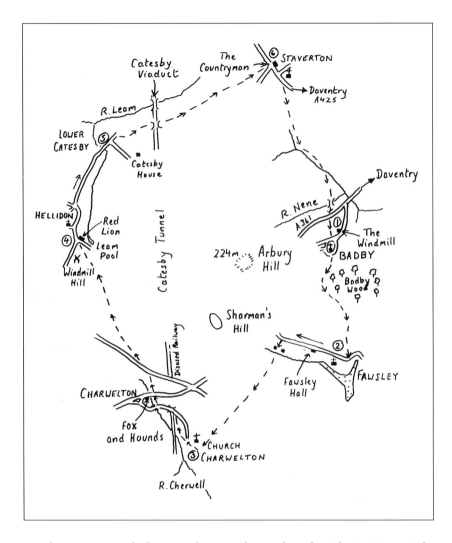

another green and the Youth Hostel standing beside it. Bear right uphill around the front of the church, where a 'Footpath to Fawsley' heads you off to the left between the walls. You are now on the 'Knightley Way', one of Northamptonshire's earliest long-distance paths, and your route to Fawsley is clearly marked over fields and along the edge of Badby Woods. Soon, on the descent, you can see handsome Fawsley Hall, now converted to private dwellings, and the attractive parkland and lakes, landscaped by Capability Brown.

2. On reaching the narrow tarmacked road, turn right. The Knightley Way soon turns off to pass the little grey church where there are many memorials to the Knightley family. Continue on the road past Fawsley Hall and other houses until a stone farm is reached as the road corners right. Here a bridleway sign directs you to the left on a stony track across the field. Pass an old stone farmhouse and continue ahead through the fields on the well-marked bridleway. The flat-topped hill immediately to your right here is Sharman's Hill – the just-superior Arbury is behind it to the right – but you will get a better view later. After crossing a minor road, the finger-post points you obliquely left, but take no notice! Continue ahead beside the fence to pass between the farm buildings and have a fine view of the church amid the sheep-fields at Church Charwelton.

3. Here you join the Jurassic Way and journey on through the churchyard. The fields around the church are the site of a village deserted in medieval times. There is no better-marked path in the county than the Jurassic Way, and no words are necessary to direct you on the next 5 miles to Staverton!

After crossing the track of the now-disused Great Central Railway, the next village you reach is Charwelton, where the Cherwell rises at Charwelton Farm. Before reaching the river, the path crosses a field on the right. Here a plank bridge takes you over a tributary before meeting the full-blown river at what was once its first crossing place, the tiny packhorse bridge. Should you already be in need of resuscitation, the Fox and Hounds is a few yards away to the left on the A361! Across the road, there are more deserted village remains in the next field. Now on a minor road, you turn left for about 80 yards before entering fields again. The waymarking is excellent and on the climb up Windmill Hill the wide views extend with every step. Over the brow, the houses, church and hostelry at Hellidon are a most attractive sight as you come down the hill!

4. Hellidon is the birthplace of the River Leam – it arises in the basement of Leam House, which stands just below the pub. Behind the house you can see Leam Pool where the water is first held back. When you are ready to continue on your journey, turn from the pub into the village, and then immediately bear right along Stockwell Lane, signed 'Village Only'. Continue on this road and at its end, turn right on the gated road to Lower Catesby.

5. Just before reaching Lower Catesby, the road crosses over the young River Leam. The village is now just a few buildings beside the road and a little church. At one time there was a priory on this site. Do not turn towards Catesby House, the large grey building on the hillside to the east, but rather keep ahead on the gravelled track and shortly look again for the Jurassic Way fossil signs directing you diagonally across a field on the right. Soon there are good views of the Catesby Viaduct over the River Leam. Continue to be guided by the signs, going under the railway track and on over the fields to Staverton.

6. The Countryman is opposite as you arrive at the main road. Take a moment to glimpse that menu! Now leave the Jurassic way and turn right on the road towards the roundabout. Opposite the church, a wooden footpath sign points you to the right into the field. Across the field there is quite a clear track winding between conifers, and the way then crosses a stony track and heads downhill across a field in a most attractive valley. A second field is crossed diagonally and the route continues by leaving the track and bearing left beside a ditch (do not cross it) in which flow the earliest waters of the Nene. The little brook is joined by another, and after keeping beside it through a large field, in the next field a wooden plank bridge allows you to cross to the other side. Cross this field diagonally to the far hedge, and then cut across the lower right corner of the next field to a waymarked stile in the hedge on the right. Cross the next field to the far hedge and follow it to the left. At the bottom of the slope the last of the three infant rivers is crossed before climbing to the road. Cross the main road and enter the field opposite. Here look for a stile in the hedge on the right. Once over this, turn left and continue following the waymarks to come out on the roadside in Badby, where just to the left you will be more than pleased to see the Windmill.

PLACES OF INTEREST NEARBY

If it should be a very clear day, you could drive around to the *Telecom tower* and test out its claim to provide a view of the Malverns. Or, if you are really into views, there is a country park in the *Burton Hills* near Fenny Compton (10 miles west) which specialises in them. Otherwise a quiet recovery in one of the aforementioned hostelries is recommended!

CANAL AND RIVER AT NETHER HEYFORD

Those two great waterways of Northamptonshire, the Grand Union Canal and the River Nene, run parallel courses for a while before meeting at Weedon, and making possible this most watery of circuits!

The Grand Union Canal near Flore

Where exactly is the centre of England – the place which is farthest from any coast? Not least among the claimants to this distinction is Weedon – or to give it its full title, Weedon Bec. Certainly the government at the time of the Napoleonic Wars seems to have thought so, since it was here that they planned to hide George III should the French have invaded, and here that they built a huge military barracks – but again, of course, the recent arrival of the Grand Junction Canal from London could have influenced their decision! Here then, in the very centre of England, is the meeting place of the Grand Union Canal and the River Nene. To be accurate, they never do meet, but rather cross, as the canal is carried high over the river on an aqueduct. On this walk, you can journey beside the canal to their crossing place, look down on the tiny river below, and then follow its meandering course through the fields and the pretty and historic village of Flore to return to Nether Heyford.

The Grand Union (the Grand Junction was its forerunner) is the most popular canal of the Inland Waterways system. In summer it is busy to say the least, but even in the depths of winter you will find boats on the move to add colour to your walk. The boats are all pleasure craft now, but this was once the most important of working canals. The past is everywhere – wharfs once used for loading iron ore or delivering coal, buildings of former boatyards, an old milepost, the remains of an old swingbridge and plenty more before reaching Weedon embankment. The Nene leads you home on a rather quieter route through lush meadows of grazing cattle.

In Middle Street, leading off the green, is the Olde Sun inn. You can't miss it – the outside has a bright-blue-painted range of old farm machinery, and, in summer, a wonderful floral display. Inside, the low-ceilinged rooms house a thousand gleaming brass ornaments, large and small. The menu is extensive and meals are good, with grills being particularly popular. There is a good range of ales, including guest ales.

Telephone: 01327 340164.

- **HOW TO GET THERE:** Nether Heyford lies just south of the A45, 3 miles west of Northampton.
- **PARKING:** The Olde Sun has parking for patrons. Otherwise there are plenty of quiet roadsides, possibly beside the green.
- **LENGTH OF THE WALK:** $5^1/_2$ miles. Map: OS Landranger 152 Northampton and Milton Keynes (GR 661586).

THE WALK

1. From the Olde Sun, walk down Middle Street to the green and turn right, following alongside the green under the lime trees. At the end of the green, turn left (signposted Stowe) and continue to the canal bridge where you turn right on to the towpath. This place was once the site of Heyford Wharf where iron ore was brought by tramway to feed the furnaces on the canalside in the middle 1800s. Soon the canal begins to curve as it winds its way along the contours around Stowe Hill. A narrowing of the canal is seen where

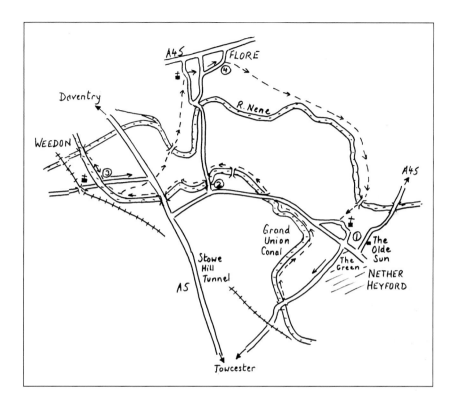

a swingbridge once crossed, and beside the white house, there is an old milestone, now newly painted. Past Bridge 29 is a boatyard which was once an old coal wharf unloading coal for the nearby villages. The little brick Bridge 28 shows the grooves of old towropes on its iron rims.

2. At Bridge 27, Flore Lane Wharf, the canal turns sharply right, a difficult corner to navigate. The tall house here was once a pub in the canal's heyday. Continuing, you pass Stowe Hill Marine, now a boatbuilding yard on the site of former lime kilns, and then the roar of the A5 intrudes upon your peace as you walk beneath it. At Bridge 25, the Nene Way leaves the towpath, and if you do not wish to walk out on Weedon embankment, you could follow the signs to the A5 crossing. Otherwise, continue ahead on the embankment to where the tiny River Nene passes underneath. After a night of heavy rain in October 1939 the canal breached at this place and millions of gallons of water from the long pound fell into the river. Standing here you can imagine all that water, and the severe flooding that resulted in Weedon and indeed all the way into Northampton.

Retrace your steps on the towpath, and after crossing above a road, look out for some steps to take you down to join it. Almost opposite, you will see St Peter's church across the canal and may be able to identify the creature on its weather vane – a goose! Apparently, back in Saxon times, Weedon was plagued by wild geese eating the crops and the locals persecuted them. They were reproached by the King's daughter, St Werburgh, who performed a miracle here in bringing a dead goose back to life. In gratitude, the geese vowed never again to graze in Weedon. (I hope you don't see any transgressors!)

3. Walk down the steps to the road, and turn right along the road to meet the A5. Cross straight over it and follow the Nene Way signs alongside a stream, over it, and then over the main river to climb to the church at Flore. Flore is a pretty village with many thatched cottages – one of these is the regular quarry of transatlantic visitors, as it was the home of the parents of John Adams, the second president of the USA, whose son, John Quincey Adams became sixth President. From the churchyard, the Nene Way turns right past the playing field and continues along Nether Lane. Where the road swings left, you are directed ahead between curious 'wattle and daub' thatched walls.

4. Now the way crosses the peaceful fields beside the winding river. At one point you pass the old Heyford Mill, now crumbling into ruin. The waymarking is good, and after a stretch close to the river, you cross it on a footbridge and return alongside the gardens into Nether Heyford. At the road, turn left through the churchyard, and then leave the Nene Way, turning right up the street to reach the green again.

PLACES OF INTEREST NEARBY
Two miles from Nether Heyford is the *Old Dairy Farm* at Upper Stowe. Here you have the rather odd but interesting mixture of a pet farm for children and craft centre shopping for adults. There is also an excellent restaurant. Telephone: 01327 340525.

WALK 8

THE BODDINGTONS AND THEIR RESERVOIR

Boddington Reservoir, created some 200 years ago to supply water for the Oxford Canal, provides you with an excellent short walk around its pleasant shores, with views of distant hills and the antics of the local sailing club to entertain you.

Boddington Reservoir

Nudging Northamptonshire's western borders, Boddington Reservoir is a tranquil stretch of water set in the hilly landscape of the Northamptonshire Heights. This is a quiet place, an out-of-the-way corner of the county, seemingly untouched by time. Farming is traditional here, the hills are still clothed in a patchwork of small fields. In the ancient hedgerows between you can find dogwood and field maple - and the rare Midland thorn! The first disturbance of this rural idyll must have come at the end of the 18th century with the construction of the Oxford Canal. Suddenly coal-carrying barges from the Midlands were moving across the peaceful plains. The canal was heavily used, and reservoirs were needed to supply the summit with extra water. Three were built, the largest of which was at Boddington.

The nearby twin villages of Upper and Lower Boddington are aptly named, since the land falls some 30 metres between them. At Upper Boddington the 15th-century church has commanding views across the plains. Each village has an excellent pub – perhaps you can find time to visit both!

At Upper Boddington, the Plough is an old thatched cottage dating from around 1550. Inside, it is simply different. The bar is old, with stone floor and low beams – and papered with newspaper cuttings from around the world. The lounge is something between an antiques shop and a front parlour from the 1930s. The food, you might expect, would be steak and kidney pudding or rabbit pie followed by jam roly-poly. Not a bit of it! Fettucine, tagliatelli, balti, rainbow trout and a most exotic range of vegetarian dishes – try Provençale Nut Wellington. There are ales to match – served in tankards, of course! Food is served every day except Sunday. Telephone: 01327 260364.

Perhaps a little less unusual, the tiny Carpenters Arms at Lower Boddington is a simple, homely pub with a cottagey feel and friendly owners. The menu is standard 'pub grub', but good – with particularly interesting mix-and-match sundae desserts. This is a Hook Norton inn with a good range of beers and ales. Excellent value, too. Please note food is not served on Mondays. Telephone: 01327 260451.

- **HOW TO GET THERE:** From the A361 Daventry-Banbury road, turn west at Byfield, signposted to Upper Boddington. The reservoir is 1 mile along on the left hand side.
- **PARKING:** There is a car park just before the reservoir. However, both pubs are happy for customers to park while taking the walk. (These friendly pubs both said they did not mind patrons bringing their own sandwiches as well!) The walk is described starting from the reservoir – but, of course, you can start from either pub.
- **LENGTH OF THE WALK:** There are several options, but the circuit of the reservoir alone is about 1½ miles. The distance is approximately doubled if you extend the walk to visit both villages. Map: OS Landranger 151 Stratford-upon-Avon (GR 497534).

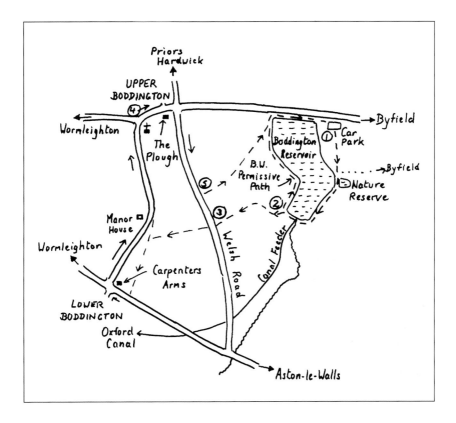

THE WALK

1. From the car park, walk away from the road and cross the stile beside the metal gate. The broad track leads you on past the sailing club, where it suddenly narrows and dives into a tunnel of trees. At the far side of this is a little bridge where the reedy pool on your left is a Northamptonshire Wildlife Trust Nature Reserve. Continuing on through the trees, and bearing right around the water, you reach the dam at the south end of the reservoir.

2. At the far end of the dam you have a choice. You can complete the circuit by turning right along the reservoir edge on a British Waterways permissive path which then takes you back to the north wall and the car park. If you wish to visit the villages – and also to get some excellent views – you should now leave the reservoir and climb uphill to the wooden kissing gate ahead. Once through this,

41

bear right diagonally uphill across the field to where a tall ash tree stands on the horizon. At the ash tree, bear left and follow the track beside the hedge to the road. There are fine views behind you all the way. The telecommunications tower which dominates the scene is perched at a height of 222 metres – just 3 metres below the county's highest point. From there, on a clear day, it is possible to see the Malvern Hills across the Warwickshire Plain.

3. Cross the road following the footpath sign opposite. Cross the field directly to a stile which leads you into another large field. Keep straight ahead, downhill, to the kissing gate at the bottom right-hand corner of the field. Through this, you are on a bridleway, and again have choices. Turning right, in about 200 metres you will arrive opposite the Manor House on the road between the Boddingtons, and will be able to continue by turning right on the road to Upper Boddington. But if you want to walk through Lower Boddington – perhaps to visit the pub or see some of the old houses – turn left and continue to the road. Once there, turn right and keep ahead to the road junction with the Carpenters Arms on the corner. Here you turn right and walk uphill on the road to Upper Boddington. There are fine views across the Warwickshire Plain as you go.

4. Passing the village shop and school, you arrive at a road junction where a house stands curiously alone on an island surrounded by roads. Turn right and pass The Plough (but it's well worth a stop) before reaching a crossroads. Turn right here. The road you are now on is known as Welsh Road and its route can be traced across many miles of country. It was the route once used by Welsh drovers, taking their cattle to fetch higher prices in the markets of London.

5. After about 1/2 mile, turn left at the first bridleway sign, and cross the field diagonally, passing a spinney of horse chestnut trees. On reaching the hedge corner at the brow of the hill, continue ahead, keeping the hedge on your left as you go down. There are excellent views over the reservoir and surrounding hills. The spire ahead to your right is that of Byfield. The track now curves left and descends through the next field with the hedge on the right. Keeping to it, you bear left around the bottom of the field and come out at a small car park beside the reservoir. Climb the steps and walk along the wall to return to the start.

The Plough inn at Upper Boddington

There is just one bonus before you leave. If you are interested in that rare Midland thorn, there are specimens in the hedgerow across the road from the north wall and up towards Upper Boddington. The leaves and flowers are slightly larger than those of the common hawthorn, but it is not easy to tell the difference – except when there are berries. The Midland thorn has two, or even three, seeds inside instead of one.

PLACES OF INTEREST NEARBY

Burton Hills Country Park is 6 miles to the east. There are some truly excellent views from here. Rather nearer to home, if the day is clear, consider driving up to that telecommunications tower. Is it really possible to see the Malverns?

For other unsophisticated pleasures, you could turn up the A361 to Fawsley or Badby. *Fawsley Park* was landscaped by Capability Brown and you have free access to picnic spots beside the lake and the tiny church with its fine carved pews, priceless stained glass and many memorials. At Badby, the *bluebell woods* in springtime should be classed as one of the seven wonders of Northamptonshire (could you suggest the other six?). If the time is right, go!

CHIPPING WARDEN AND THE RIVER CHERWELL

This easy walk beginning in one of Northamptonshire's most attractive villages, follows the infant River Cherwell through a pretty wooded valley near the county's western border.

Edgecote Pool

The River Cherwell makes just a short journey through Northamptonshire, but the countryside through which it passes is arguably some of the finest in the county. The little river arises at Cherwell Farm above the village of Charwelton and continues through the lovely villages of Church Charwelton and Woodford Halse before turning west and heading for the county boundary and its final meeting with the Thames at Oxford. Here below Chipping Warden the river flows through fields of grazing sheep and cattle, its willow-lined banks shaded by tall poplars. Its waters feed The Pool at Edgecote House, a silvery stretch of water in the landscaped grounds of a fine mansion dating from the 1700s. The former house on this site, since destroyed by fire, gave refuge to Charles I and his retinue the night before the Battle of Edgehill in 1642.

Chipping Warden itself is a delight. Its beauty is in the stone – a glorious deep-coloured sandy ironstone which glows in the sunshine and imparts an air of warmth in any weather. Many of the houses are thatched and most display a riot of summer flowers. The 14th-century church is beautifully set beside a well-kept green where stands the huge base of an old market cross.

Beside one of the greens at Chipping Warden is the Griffin – a fine old pub of local stone, bedecked with flowers and creepers. Inside it is very much a local with a good range of real ales and interestingly, an assortment of country wines and punches on offer. The menu is standard, but very good value. Telephone: 01295 660230. Should you really fancy something different, the other pub in Chipping Warden, the Rose and Crown, (telephone 01295 660850), while again looking much of a local, turns out to be concealing a Chinese and Thai restaurant in its back rooms! The choice is yours.

- **HOW TO GET THERE:** Chipping Warden lies on the A361, 4 miles north of Banbury.
- **PARKING:** Both pubs offer parking for patrons, but it is also possible to park on the quiet roadside near the church (follow the 'Village Only' sign).
- **LENGTH OF THE WALK:** 3½ miles, but a shorter 1½ mile option is possible. Map: OS Landranger 151 Stratford-upon-Avon (GR 499487).

THE WALK

1. From the church, walk down the road and pass between the two stone pillars at the entrance to the estate. This stony track was once the drive to Edgecote House. It continues downhill with pleasant views and crosses the Cherwell on an attractive stone and ironwork bridge. Climbing again, the track emerges on the road in front of the House and you can admire the elegant buildings and the fine old church beside them.

2. If you are feeling a short walk is enough for today, turn right on this road, and on meeting the 'main' road at its bend, turn right on the marked bridleway. This will lead you again over the Cherwell

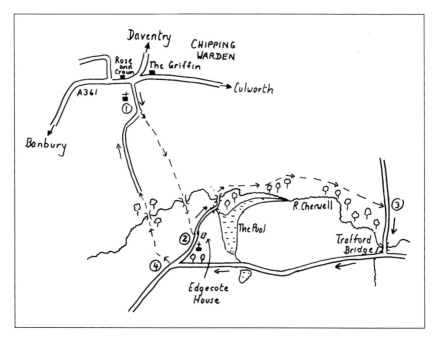

(there is a pleasantly shaded picnic spot beside the bridge) and back to Chipping Warden.

To continue with the main walk, turn left on the road in front of Edgecote House. The road dips past the stables and crosses in front of a house which was once a mill – the water from Edgecote Pool is here spilling over into the river. Cross two bridges, the first over the old mill stream and the second over the Cherwell itself. Now turn right and soon the river bends to come beside the track again. Here bear right alongside the river and head for a waymarked gate with woodland beyond. After passing the woodland, you reach a field where the path initially keeps to the left-hand hedge. At the bottom of the field, the reedy tip of Edgecote Pool can be seen and the Cherwell is hurrying across to once again hide itself in the trees. When you reach a track from the farm on the left, leave the left-hand hedge and bear right across the field, aiming to the left of the line of poplars ahead. Here a waymarked stile leads you over a tiny stream, after which the path bears right around the woodland edge. In the next field, continue with the woodland on your right and leave through a waymarked gate in the right-hand fence. Crossing the corner of the next field brings you to the road.

Edgecote House

3. Turn right on the road and walk down to the corner at Trafford Bridge. Take the road to the right just after the bridge and keep to this to return to Edgecote. It is a very quiet road and will afford you some excellent views. The river can be seen winding through the woodland below and soon the other side of Edgecote House comes into view. There are glimpses of Edgecote Pool through the trees and at one point an attractive pond on the left also.

4. When you reach the corner with Edgecote House on the right, leave the road and keep straight ahead on the bridleway. This goes downhill beside the hedge, and once more in woodland, crosses the rushing Cherwell on a tiny bridge. Before the bridge, a huge beech and chestnut compete to shade a riverside spot seemingly designed for picnicking. Over the bridge, the track continues uphill, and soon becomes a concrete road which returns you to Chipping Warden.

PLACES OF INTEREST NEARBY
Just 4 miles away is the village of *Middleton Cheney*. Here the unexpected treat is in the church – a most remarkable collection of 19th-century stained glass windows by William Morris. A leaflet is available to guide you round.

WHITFIELD AND
THE GREAT OUSE

Here is a short walk in an attractive and little-known corner of the county. Following the infant Great Ouse through parkland and quiet pastures, you return over the hill to the pretty village of Whitfield and its rather surprising hostelry!

One of several pools seen on the walk

From ancient times, rivers have fixed the borders of territory – a line of defence which cannot easily be breached. Much of Northamptonshire's boundary is river – the Leam separates the county from Warwickshire, the Avon separates it from Leicestershire and the Welland from both Leicestershire and Rutland. In the south, the Tove and the Great Ouse form the boundary with Buckinghamshire, and the Cherwell the boundary with Oxfordshire. It is interesting to note that each of these rivers arises within Northamptonshire. No wonder the county once thought itself the highest place in England! Here in the far south of the county, the walk follows the Great Ouse along the Buckinghamshire border near Whitfield. The river arises on the high ground north of Brackley and flows some 140 miles past Bedford and Ely on its way to the Wash near King's Lynn. It has the distinction of being Britain's fifth longest river, longer than the Wye or the Nene. But here it is just a baby, spending its early days wandering through gentle farmland, and crossing the pleasant wooded parkland of Biddlesden House, where its watery pools abound with heron and wildfowl. When your path leaves the waterside, a short climb over the hill gives long views of Oxfordshire and Buckinghamshire before descending to the little village of Whitfield where an interesting old inn awaits.

The Sun is an old stone building tucked away in a quiet corner of the village. Outside, all is white tables and bright flowers. The inside approximates to Aladdin's Cave! With low-beamed ceilings hung with copper and pewter and foliage draped densely around the bar, the walls are most originally papered with the world's bank notes, interspersed with sheets of irridescent colour bearing the menu. It will take you a long time to read it all. Suffice it to say that you can get everything from a fried egg sandwich to a whole lobster, with quite a lot in between. The Sun is a freehouse, and there is a good range of beers and real ales to accompany your meal. And the value is exceptional! Only one word of caution. Don't choose a Monday lunchtime when no food is served.

Telephone: 01280 850232.

- **HOW TO GET THERE:** Whitfield lies just off the A43, 2 miles north-east of Brackley.
- **PARKING:** On roadsides in the village, or, for patrons, at The Sun.
- **LENGTH OF THE WALK:** 4 miles. Map: OS Landranger 152 Northampton and Milton Keynes (GR 607395).

THE WALK

1. From The Sun, walk on down the village street, away from the A43. Leaving the village, the road descends to cross the tiny river beside an old mill, now converted into a most attractive property with watery gardens. You are now in Buckinghamshire. Continuing a short distance along the road to some stone farm buildings, turn left beside the river, following the wooden footpath sign. Leave this riverside field via a stile, and enter the next field via another,

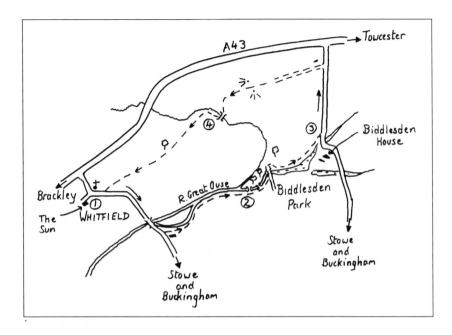

keeping the river on your left. A stile at the far end of this field leads you on. Waymarks are absent, but the stiles will guide you on your way. In the large field, which may be a little overgrown, continue on the track which bears right along the hedge and bank (the river is still to your left) and at the end keep ahead on a track between the hedges. After passing a game enclosure on the left, the track leads on to another stile where you enter a huge open field with the woodland of Biddlesden Park on the far side. Turn left and follow the left hand fence above the wooded banks of the river.

2. About halfway along the field, a stile and a gate in the left-hand fence lead to a wooden bridge over the river. The riverside here is very pretty, but your path continues ahead along the edge of the field, keeping the river on your left. The river bank is wooded, and through the trees can be seen pools which seem very popular with wildfowl. Keeping straight ahead, you reach a stony lane leading from Biddlesden House, and here you should turn left and cross over the river to enter a large park field. Here at last there is a waymark directing you to bear slightly left across the field. But the true path is along the right hand edge beside the river! The several pools here are most attractive, and again wildfowl and herons abound. Biddlesden House is now well concealed behind the trees on the right - the site on which it is built was that of a Cistercian abbey dissolved by Henry VIII. Leaving the field through a gateway beside the river, you continue in the next field to a gate in the right-hand hedge leading to a road.

3. Turn left on the road, and follow it uphill for nearly ½ mile to where a bridleway leads off on the left before some barns. The broad bridleway now leads on, climbing slightly with increasing distant views ahead. Eventually a field is reached, and the bridleway is no more. Continue along the side of the field with the hedge to your right to enter the next field. Again keep the hedge on your right (but detour around the disused pit!) and continue to the corner of the field. Now turn left and descend, looking out for a stile in the hedge on your right before the bottom of the field. It is well hidden, and leads to an even better concealed plank bridge behind.

4. Now turn right along the edge of the field, and keeping the stream on your right, continue through (or over) the gate into the next field. There are no waymarks here, but you are on a public footpath. Bear left uphill across this huge field, heading just to the left of a group of trees on the horizon. When you arrive there, you will find the gate beside the trees waymarked. Following the arrow direction, walk straight across this next big field (which may contain cattle – beware if you have a dog with you). At the far side, a stile beside a gate leads you through a small paddock and out into a lane. Turn left on the lane and then right along the village street to reach The Sun.

PLACES OF INTEREST NEARBY
Stowe Landscape Gardens, are situated about 5 miles east of Whitfield. Continue on the minor road through the village and turn right at the T-junction. Owned by the National Trust, they have been dubbed 'Britain's largest work of art'. Scattered in the vast landscaped grounds of Stowe School is an amazing assortment of Georgian monuments – temples, bridges, arches, columns and many others, with more restoration still going on. Opening hours vary with seasons, school terms and the weather, so it is well worth phoning first. Telephone: 01280 822850.

COSGROVE AND THE IRON TRUNK

At Cosgrove the Grand Union Canal is dramatically carried over the River Ouse on a high aqueduct known as the Iron Trunk, while in the attractive valley below the Great Ouse winds its reedy way through banks of willow.

The Iron Trunk

The building of the Grand Junction (now Grand Union) Canal at the very end of the 18th century changed life for ever in those communities on its route. This was certainly the case at Cosgrove, where a huge embankment was built to carry the canal through the heart of the village. The village street was cut in two, and left-bank dwellers would never again have been able to communicate with those of the right had someone not thought to cut a narrow passage underneath! To cope with wider traffic, a most ornate Gothic-style stone bridge was built over the canal further up and village connections were fully reinstated! The whole canal from London to Birmingham was opened in 1800, but here in Cosgrove there were still troubles. An aqueduct had been planned to cross the Ouse valley, but it was not finished and seven temporary locks were put in to carry the canal down to the river and up again. The aqueduct at Cosgrove was in fact the last part of the Grand Junction Canal to be completed and it finally opened to traffic in 1805. Leaks occurred almost immediately, and after repair, there was even more drama when the arches of the aqueduct collapsed one February night, blocking the river and threatening to flood nearby Wolverton. The temporary locks were again used while a cast iron 'trunk' was ordered and finally installed in 1811. It is still in use today, standing on brick pillars 35 feet above the River Ouse.

The walk takes you across this masterpiece of engineering, and then underneath it through a 'cattle-creep', created to connect the fields on either side. Beyond is the Ouse Valley Park, a flat land where the river rolls sluggishly through dense beds of reeds, watched over by silent grazing cattle. The old Wolverton Mill stands in a picturesque setting, and further on you reach a wetland conservation area around pits once used for gravel extraction. At Old Stratford you turn back, and crossing fields arrive once again beside a canal – or rather the remains of one, since the Stratford and Buckingham Canal has now been out of water for some 50 years. Built at the time of the Grand Junction, it was never much of a commercial success, its main cargo being hay for the cab-horses of London. Waterways enthusiasts have campaigned for its restoration, but it is too late. The A5 by-pass is now built across its bed and we shall never see it in its former glory. But you can enjoy a walk along the old towpath under the trees and appreciate the wealth of vegetation in its overgrown bed which must be a sanctuary for wildlife in this cultivated landscape.

When you arrive back in Cosgrove, you can take the tunnel to return to the Barley Mow – just as the canal horses once did, to reach the stabling provided for them at the inn. The pub is older than the canal – and still derives a lot of its trade from water travellers. Consequently it is open all day on summer weekends, and specialises in hearty meals such as steaks – of beef, gammon, turkey or salmon. But there are also sandwiches, ploughman's and other light snacks, and all can be eaten in the pleasant canalside garden (with large play area) where you can observe the comings and goings on this lively stretch of canal.

Telephone: 01908 562957.

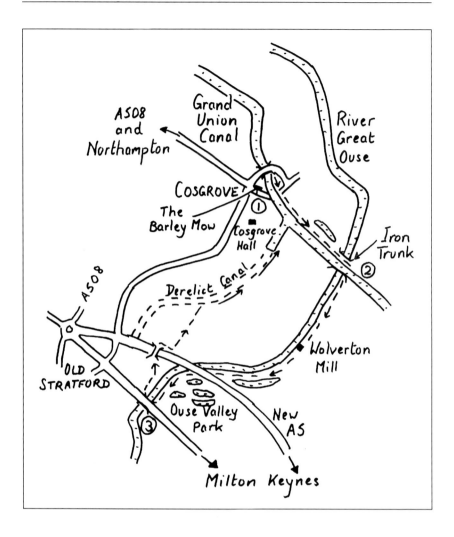

- **HOW TO GET THERE:** Cosgrove lies ½ mile off the A508, just north of Milton Keynes.
- **PARKING:** The Barley Mow is pleased to offer parking to its patrons, but you can also park on quiet roadsides.
- **LENGTH OF THE WALK:** 4½ miles. Map: OS Landranger 152 Northampton and Milton Keynes (GR 793426).

THE WALK

1. From the Barley Mow, return to the crossroads, and turn right.

The road through the village soon crosses the canal, and here you turn right to descend to the towpath. Behind you there is a good view of that fine old stone bridge. Ahead of you the canal swings in an arc to reach the junction with the old Buckingham Arm and Cosgrove Lock. This is a lively spot at any time of year, but most especially so in summer. The Grand Union is busy and there are usually boats queuing on both sides to use the lock. Their bright colours and traditional painting make an attractive scene. To the right are the grounds of Georgian Cosgrove Hall and in front of them the Buckingham Arm, this end of which is now used as a marina. As you continue ahead to the Iron Trunk, below you on the left are the lakes of a leisure park, created after gravel was extracted for the building of the M1.

2. After crossing the Iron Trunk, turn left down the slope and double-back to pass under the aqueduct through the cattle-creep. Now keep to the tarmacked path beside the River Ouse, which is here the county boundary. You are, in fact, in Buckinghamshire! It is a pleasant and easy walk across these meadows to reach the old Wolverton Mill which is now being converted and restored. Cross straight over the track here, following the fingerpost to Stony Stratford. The path enters the Ouse Valley Park and leads on beside the river, past reed beds and bulrushes, moorhens and swans. When nearing the A5, do not pass under the arches, but go through a gate on the right and continue along the riverside. Soon the river swings, and you cross beside it under the A5 overpass. Now the track winds on beside a wetland conservation area, again created from gravel-working sites. It is beautifully kept, and all too soon you arrive at the gate at its end, beside the old stone bridge which carries the road which was once Watling Street across the Ouse.

3. Turn right on the road, and cross over the bridge. A few yards along on the far side, a footpath sign points off on the right. Following this, you soon cross a field, and then skirt a new housing estate to reach a footbridge over the A5. On the far side of this road, keep right along the hedge, and then bear left downhill through a waymarked gateway. Cross the field ahead directly to a bridge and stile on the far side. Now, following the waymarks, climb gently uphill to reach the trees which line the route of the old Buckingham Canal, and turn right on to its towpath. The place is still and quiet, and you

Ouse Valley Park, Cosgrove

can almost hear the creaking of the ropes and thud of the horses' hooves as they hauled the barges full of hay. After mounting a slight rise, it is a surprise to come upon a canal full of water and boats galore, people and dogs, bikes, washing, barbecues and all the activity of a marina. Still keeping to the towpath, you shortly reach the Grand Union, where you can cross over the lock gates to regain the towpath on which you set out. Turn left now back to Cosgrove, but just opposite the old buildings, turn right down the steps, and return to the Barley Mow by way of the old village street under the canal.

PLACES OF INTEREST NEARBY

There is much of interest in Cosgrove itself. The trip boat *Linda* makes 2 hour trips down the canal to New Bradwell on weekends in summer. This wonderful old boat once belonged to the famous carrying company Fellows, Morton and Clayton, and she had the distinction of carrying the Queen Mother in 1964 at the reopening of the Stratford Canal.

Cosgrove Leisure Park can be reached by continuing on the road after crossing the canal bridge. It offers picnic and play areas, swimming pool and tennis court, fishing lakes, restaurant and shops, all for a modest entrance fee.

BLISWORTH TUNNEL FROM MILTON MALSOR

Leaving Milton Malsor the Grand Union is surprisingly peaceful, despite the proximity of road and railway. After winding attractively around the back gardens of Blisworth it enters a deep green cutting which ends in the famous Blisworth Tunnel, the longest on the inland waterways.

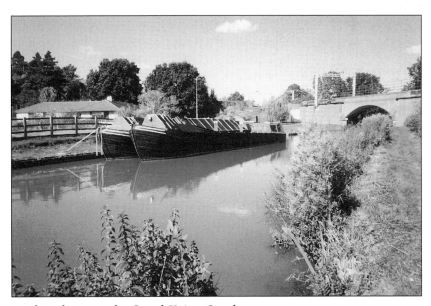

Working boats on the Grand Union Canal

The opening of the Grand Junction Canal from Braunston to London in 1800 was an event of some importance. Formerly coal from the Midlands had been brought down by the narrow winding Oxford Canal and then transferred into lighters which carried it on down the Thames. Now the journey was cut by 60 miles – three days travel – and no transhipment would be needed. On opening day there remained just one problem still to be solved, just one small gap in the route – the hill above Blisworth. Work had started on a tunnel here six years earlier, but the geology of the planes of porous rock had not been correctly judged and the tunnel had flooded with water. The best canal engineers of the day had been called in and after much wrangling and deliberating, they had decided to build a temporary horse railway across Blisworth Hill, loading and unloading cargoes at each end. It was to be a further five long years before a tunnel was completed from Blisworth to Stoke Bruerne and such was the excitement then that 5,000 people turned out to greet the first boat through.

The tunnel had no towpath, so horses went over the top along the route of the old railway. The boats were taken through by registered 'leggers', hired from the canal company, who lay on boards and walked sideways on the walls. Since the tunnel is 3,076 yards – almost two miles – in length, this was exhausting work! Today's boats take about half an hour to go through, and Blisworth is the longest tunnel still in use on the waterways.

Backing on to the village green at Milton Malsor, the Greyhound is a Chef and Brewer pub serving 'home-cooked food, all day, every day, 8 days a week'. Inside, the pub is a warren of small rooms, each with low beams and dark wooden furniture, pewter mugs and dried flowers. To say the menu is extensive would be an understatement – expect to spend about half an hour browsing around the chalk boards. The time is reduced if you opt for the snack menu, which is also very popular. There is a fine choice of real ales, beers and wines to accompany your meal.

Telephone: 01604 858449.

- **HOW TO GET THERE:** Milton Malsor lies 2 miles south of Northampton, and can be reached by turning where signposted from the ring road to the south or from the A43.
- **PARKING:** There is plenty of parking for patrons at the Greyhound. Alternatively, park on a quiet roadside in the village.
- **LENGTH OF THE WALK:** 5½ miles. Add another 4 miles if you wish to continue to see the tunnel end at Stoke Bruerne. Map: OS Landranger 152 Northampton and Milton Keynes (GR 733557).

THE WALK

1. From the Greyhound, turn left on the main road, and then right at the Rothersthorpe turn. Follow the road to the bottom of the hill, where a fingerpost directs you across a field on the left. Cross the

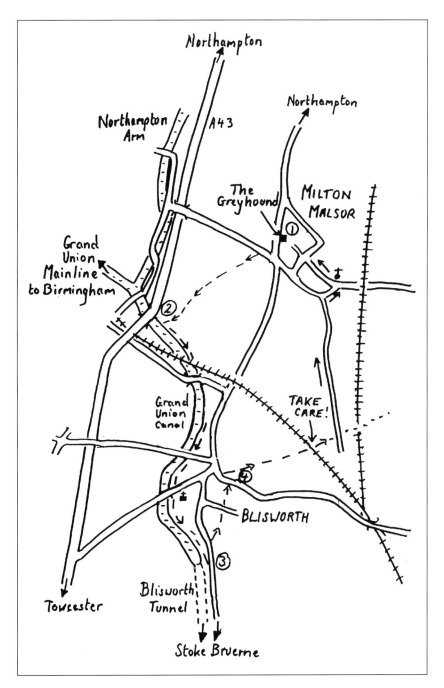

first and second fields diagonally on a usually well-cut path between crops. The path goes on across another field, now heading south, and at the next hedge a fine stile-and-plank bridge takes you across the stream. Coming close to the A43, you pass behind a filling station on the right, after which a hedge is reached. Immediately before the hedge, another good plank bridge crosses a stream. In the field on the far side, head diagonally across towards the tip of a hedge below the road, where a stile will lead you into a cutting. Now bear slightly left uphill on the path leading to the top of the cutting. A few yards after reaching the top, turn right on a track which runs downhill towards the brick road bridge. After passing through a gate, the track bears left to join the canal towpath.

2. Turn left on the towpath (the junction with the Northampton Arm is under the bridges on your right). The noise of the A43 recedes as you go, and after the railway bridge you are on a quiet stretch of rural canal often chosen as a winter base by those who make their homes on the water. The canal winds on towards the houses and church at Blisworth, sheltering on their hillside. After the attractive Bridge 50 you have the gardens of Blisworth for your enjoyment and soon the boatyard base of the smart Blisworth Tunnel fleet is passed. At Bridge 51 the huge red brick building is a Victorian mill, while beside it was a Pickford transhipment depot where goods were once transferred to the horse tramway. Continuing ahead, trees overhang the canal and gradually the wooded banks close in as the tunnel approaches.

3. Just before the tunnel mouth a track leads you up to the road. If you are feeling energetic, you could turn right here and follow the road and then the marked route of the old tramway to reach the other end of the tunnel at Stoke Bruerne. On the way you can see the ventilation shafts and spoil heaps of earth dug from the tunnel in its construction. Those continuing with the main walk should turn left on the road (note the old Blisworth Stone Works building on the right) and after about 200 yards, turn right at a bridleway sign. This leads you up into some allotments, and here the track you want is the one bearing uphill to the right. After passing a footpath junction, continue to a wooden fence and then bear right around the gardens, still on the bridleway which is now a tarmacked path. Keep to this, crossing a small road, to reach a main road.

Locks at Stoke Bruerne

4. Turn left, and after 100 yards, right on a footpath signed to Collingtree (if you continue ahead here you will reach Blisworth village and the Royal Oak). Pass the playing field and leave by a waymarked stile in the hedge. There are fine views across Northampton. Walk diagonally across the field to where steps lead you up to the railway line. Trains here are fast and frequent and you should certainly take care when crossing, but visibility is good. On the far side of the line, maintaining the same direction across two fields brings you to a broad track where you should turn left to return to Milton Malsor. At its end, bear right to the church, where you turn left and then keep ahead through the village to reach the little green and across the road, the rear entrance to The Greyhound.

PLACES OF INTEREST NEARBY
A visit to the other end of the tunnel at Stoke Bruerne is recommended, where there is much more in the way of entertainment. The colourful *Canal Museum* is full of interest and the giftshop beside it has an amazing choice of waterways orientated books and painted canal ware. A trip boat leaves from the wharf, you can watch boats working through the locks, and there are pubs and teashops of every kind. Telephone: 01604 862229.

THE RIVER NENE FROM BILLING MILL

Close to Northampton, this surprisingly pretty stretch of riverside is contrasted with a climb to the lovely stone village of Little Houghton and an exhilarating walk along the Washlands dyke where sheep and wildfowl graze together.

Billing Mill

The Ice Age left its legacy to Northamptonshire! The huge glacier which slid along the Nene Valley broke the rock beneath to give some of the finest gravel in Britain. With the road-building boom of the 20th century, that gravel became very valuable and much of the valley has been subjected to the might of the excavators. Now few sites remain active, the others having been modified by man and nature to give us fishing and boating lakes, leisure areas and nature reserves. The Nene Valley has changed, but may have gained rather more than it has lost. The lakes of Billing Aquadrome, where the walk begins, are the result of early gravel extractions in the 1920s - and the vision of the then owner of the site, one Mr Mackaness. Although the site is big, the caravans dotted around scarcely intrude on the peace of the riverside and it is not unusual to glimpse a passing kingfisher. Wildfowl wander between the plots sampling one small lake after another, and are particularly delightful in early summer when many have their young families in tow. At one point you pass the very curious Clifford Hill, probably constructed by the Normans to defend the crossing of the river here. Behind Clifford Hill, from the lovely brown stone village of Little Houghton, you can look out along the length of the valley.

This walk has one more treat in store for you – the Washlands dyke. In the 1970s a huge reservoir was created to hold back the flood waters of the often swollen Nene and so protect the developments of the lower valley. A walk on the dyke is bracing and always full of interest. Migrating birds use the Washlands as a feeding station and lapwings and golden plovers overwinter here – don't forget your binoculars! The way home is again along the riverside, past the craft of Northampton boating club, and under the long line of shady poplars to the old mill beside the water.

Billing Mill was a working mill until the 1940s, and became a museum before recently being converted to a pub. Inside you can see the machinery and wheels of the old mill. Although a modern pub, the old character has been well-preserved inside and the low ceilings and heavy beams are complemented by solid wooden tables, brasses and much paraphernalia from the working mill. Outside tables abound, and life can be very pleasant on a warm sunny day here, watching the comings and goings on the river. The fare is reasonably standard, but well presented, and there are one or two more exotic dishes such as Pastitsio (a noodle dish!) or Chicken Piri Piri (hot and spicy!). The beer is from Mansfield's range, but there are other brews on offer.

Telephone: 01604 415059.

- **HOW TO GET THERE:** From the A45 on the eastern outskirts of Northampton, turn where signed to Cogenhoe and Billing. Go straight on at the roundabout and then turn beside the river and over the bridge to the mill.
- **PARKING:** There is plenty of parking beside the river and around the mill.

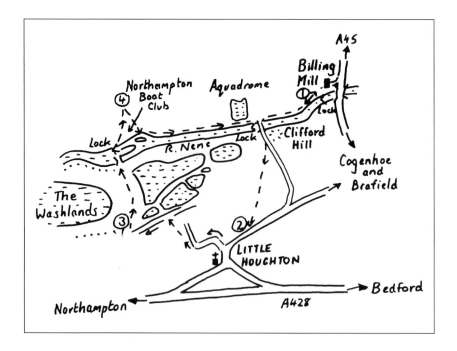

- **LENGTH OF THE WALK:** 4 miles. Map: OS Landranger 152 Northampton and Milton Keynes (GR 815612).

THE WALK

1. From Billing Mill, cross the footbridge towards the river, and then turn right along the riverside. After about ½ mile beside the winding river, Clifford Hill appears on the opposite bank. Its curious flat shape is due to the popularity of bowls some 300 years ago – the top was removed to provide a bowling green with a view for the enthusiasts of the time! Soon you reach Clifford Lock, and there cross the river. The old Clifford Mill is now the premises of a wrought iron specialist. When you reach the road beyond, Clifford Hill is behind you on the left. A footpath can be seen climbing uphill on the right towards the clustered houses of Little Houghton, and following this path, you reach the road beside the village.

2. Turn right on the road and walk into the village. The houses are of dark sandstone and ironstone and most of the village is a conservation area. At the junction, turn to the right into Meadow

Lane and head downhill. Where the road swings sharply right, follow the footpath sign uphill beside an attractive stone house. Turn right in the field, and then soon pass through a waymarked gate on your right to head downhill again. Once again there is a view of lakes and below you is the huge bowl reservoir of the Washlands Scheme. You head downhill beside a line of trees and through the gate, turn left on the lane. Continue ahead, and then uphill to reach the top of the dyke.

3. Turn right on the dyke, and follow it anti-clockwise to the sluice gate on the opposite side. Here you have the feeling of being on top of the world - no doubt exaggerated by the usually bracing breezes. Lakes and river are below you, and the green swards are dotted with sheep and grazing wildfowl. After crossing above the gates, turn down to the right and cross the footbridge beside Favell Lock. The path passes between the moorings of Northampton Boat Club and then heads up a lane away from the river.

4. After the gate at the end of the lane, turn right, and almost immediately right again, following the Nene Way signs beside a small tributary. The way goes on beside the river and under the whispering poplar trees. Opposite are the moorings and huts of the boat club and it seems that wildfowl as well as boats enjoy this sheltered backwater. Soon the boundary of the aquadrome is reached, but your path continues beside the river beneath the tall poplars. Lakes appear on the left, and still the path hugs the riverside, leaving the caravanners and their open pastures. Soon the crossing at Clifford Mill is reached, and you must retrace your steps on the river bank to return to the comforts of the restored mill at Billing.

PLACES OF INTEREST NEARBY

Billing Aquadrome has more to offer, well away from the peace of the riverside. Children will love the fun fair, mini-train, and boating lake, while on a hot day the outdoor swimming pool is justly popular. Telephone: 01604 408181.

The *Saxon Church at Earls Barton*, 3 miles down the valley, welcomes visitors from far and wide. The stone ribbing on the tower dates it around AD 970 and it is said to be one of the most important Saxon buildings in England.

AROUND PITSFORD WATER FROM HOLCOT

At the heart of the county is vast Pitsford Water with more than 13 miles of attractive shoreline. This walk starts out across the hills on the south side, from which there are many excellent views along the length of the valley, before returning beside the water's edge.

Fishing fleet on Pitsford Water

Late in the 1950s, the Valley of Three Hundred Springs was dammed and flooded to supply water for growing Northampton. Not only the springs, but several tributaries of the Nene provided the 4,000 million gallons needed to fill it. Now almost half a century on, the great sparkling stretch of water offers recreation for sailors, anglers, bird watchers, cyclists, and, not least, walkers. The curving irregularly shaped lake is divided by the causeway, the northern part with its thickly wooded shores being a nature reserve. The walk described here takes in the southern part of the reservoir and starts from the stone village of Holcot on the hill above. Keeping to the high ground for some distance, you can appreciate the contorted outline of the shore as every twist in the path seems to bring a different view. After passing through the attractive parkland of Moulton Grange, the path descends by reedy Pitsford Creek, and there follows a bracing crossing of the dam before Brixworth Country Park. The fascinating Visitor Centre here is well worth a short detour and there is an excellent snack restaurant - and even the possibility to hire a bike should you be feeling really exhausted! But the path home beside the water is most pleasant, with alternating creek and headland, woodland and open shore, before climbing the hill to Holcot where an interesting old pub awaits.

The White Swan is a pub with a history – and while you are waiting for your meal you can read about it from the inside of the menu. The slight eccentricity of the friendly owners is revealed with a grid reference and global position thrown in too! The menu is extensive for such a small pub, much is home-made, and moreover the value is excellent. For something different, try the Boerewors, a South African spicy sausage. This is a freehouse, and as such has a good range of ales, beers and wines to accompany the meal. Food is served every lunchtime and every evening except Sunday.

Telephone: 01604 781263.

- **HOW TO GET THERE:** Holcot can be reached by turning west where signed from the A43 Kettering road, 4 miles north of Northampton. To reach the causeway car park, follow the signs to Brixworth from the crossroads in Holcot village.
- **PARKING:** There is not a great deal of parking at the White Swan, but some parking on quiet roadsides elsewhere in the village is possible. There is ample parking by the causeway and at Brixworth Country Park.
- **LENGTH OF THE WALK:** 6½ miles. Maps: OS Landrangers 152 Northampton and Milton Keynes, and 141 Kettering and Corby (GR 793698).

THE WALK

The walk is described starting from the White Swan, but could equally well start from the car park beside the causeway (point 6 on the map) or Brixworth Country Park Visitor Centre (point 5 on the map).

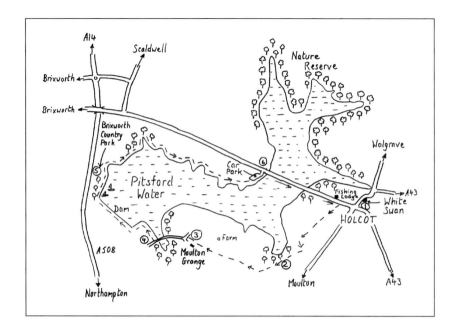

1. From the White Swan, walk uphill to the crossroads, and turn right (signposted Brixworth). Just after the last house, a fingerpost directs you across a field on the left. After crossing the stile on the opposite side of the field you have good views across the water. Continue with the fence on your left to descend to a wide plank bridge over a stream. Bear right around the bottom of a hedge, and climb again on a broad grassy track with the hedge on your left. Again there are good views – the dam and wooded shores of the Nature Reserve can be seen to the right, while Brixworth with its spire appears over the water to the left. Crossing the access road to the cricket ground, you follow the direction of the fingerpost downhill towards some horse jumps. Just before the first jump, another fingerpost directs you across a field on the left, heading away from the water. At the far side of the field, turn right beside the hedge and descend to a fine complex of wooden gates and bridge beside a green signpost on the edge of a wood.

2. Go through the gate on the left following the pointer to Pitsford and head diagonally across the field, approximately along the line of the telegraph poles. At the far side, make for some low conifers in a thicket to the left of the duck enclosure. Cross a plank bridge over a ditch, after which you cross the corner of the next field, climbing diagonally to a post at a hedge corner. After another waymarked plank bridge here, you turn left along the hedge. At the top of the field, a waymarked stile about 20 yards to the right leads you beside a glorious sweet chestnut tree into a small spinney. The path is now well waymarked, and you continue through two more similar spinneys, keeping the hedge on your left, and passing a farm on your right. Soon the cream Regency facade of Moulton Grange is seen over the hedge on the left.

3. On reaching the tarmacked road, turn left, following the waymarks. Just outside Fox Lodge, a waymark directs you to bear right on the long road through the grounds, where again you can appreciate the fine trees. On leaving through the gate, continue on the road ahead across pretty Pitsford Creek with its wildfowl.

4. Turn right through the metal gate just after the creek. The track leads you on across the dam and afterwards turns right through woodland behind the sailing club. Where the trees end, a gate on the left gives access to Brixworth Country Park and Visitor Centre, where you may appreciate a break.

5. Continuing on the perimeter path, the open shore soon gives way to Brixworth Wood. Creeks and headlands follow, and soon the tower of Holcot church is seen on its hill ahead before the causeway comes into view. At the car park it seems that every duck and swan on the water is waiting for a morsel of your lunch!

6. Turn right on the road, cross the causeway and up the hill to Holcot. Turn left at the crossroads to reach the White Swan.

PLACES OF INTEREST NEARBY

Brixworth itself has a fine old *Saxon church* dating from around AD 680 – quite possibly the oldest in England. You have been able to see its spire across the water for much of the walk.

Permits for visiting the *Nature Reserve* and its accessible hides can be obtained from the Fishing Lodge on the hill on the Holcot Road. The round walk through the reserve is about 6 miles in length.

WALK 15
LAKES IN THE NENE VALLEY AT RINGSTEAD

❦

Beside the village of Ringstead, Kinewell Lake is one of the little known treasures of the Nene Valley. More lakes, an old water-mill, stepping stones and two locks on the river complete your walk.

Kinewell Lake

Kinewell Lake is one of Northamptonshire's first 'Pocket Parks' – although it must be said, you would need quite a large pocket for this one! Kinewell is, of course, one of those lakes formed after gravel extraction. Here nature was allowed to take its course again, and after 20 years and only a little help from man, a most attractive lakeside scene has developed. The reedy shores are overhung with willow and alder, while farther back dense banks of purple willow herb are shaded by tall poplars. Water birds, butterflies and dragonflies are in their element and otters are being encouraged to return and join them. Creeks and islands offer you ever-changing views and the occasional seat is placed for you to enjoy it all. Picnic tables and a hide beside the water are also provided by the Kinewell Trust who do an admirable job in caring for this delightful place.

There are many lakes in this part of the valley, and you can see a long silvery line of them as you look down from the road above the old mill. Shortly your walk takes you down beside the nearest, Brightwells Lake, and then crosses the river close to the lake on Ringstead Island. The land around the shores of both these lakes has open access under agreement with the Countryside Commission and you may like to extend your walk. The meadow between Brightwells Lake and the river sports a fine show of wild flowers in springtime, and winter brings flocks of migrating birds. Returning to Ringstead along Station Road (the station was burned down some 60 years ago), there is yet another lake, this time a trout fishery, beside you.

If all this water has made you thirsty, there is a fine range of ales on offer at the Axe and Compass. To go with them, you have everything from toasted sandwiches at the bar to an exciting full meal in the very pleasant restaurant – the perfect end to a very watery walk!

Telephone: 01933 622227.

- **HOW TO GET THERE:** Ringstead can be reached by turning west off the A45 Wellingborough to Oundle road at Raunds. At the junction at the bottom of the hill beside the New Inn, turn left, pass the church and take the second road on the right (Carlow Road) to reach the Axe and Compass.
- **PARKING:** Walkers patronising the Axe and Compass may leave their cars there. There is also a lakeside car park which is found on the Great Addington road, just after the last houses in the village.
- **LENGTH OF THE WALK:** 3½ miles. Map: OS Landranger 141 Kettering and Corby (GR 983751).

THE WALK

1. From the lakeside car park, walk to the lake and turn right (anti-clockwise). Or if you are starting from the Axe and Compass, cross the road and walk down Meadow Close opposite. Just before its end, a footpath goes off on the left and this brings you to the lake, where again you walk to the right.

The path is quite clear all the way around the lake. Soon after the

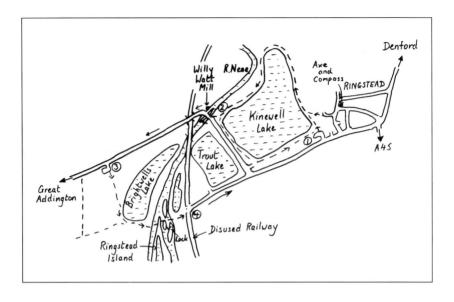

start the path becomes gravelly and hides itself from the lake behind a thick belt of trees. But it soon returns and suddenly arrives at a grassy cove where a seat awaits. Further on, you move close to the river – there is a connecting channel – and the path is shaded by tall willows. As you approach Willy Watt Mill, the scene opens out and you can admire this lovely one-time watermill beside the old stone bridge where colourful narrow boats are moored.

2. Here you leave the path beside the lake and continue ahead through the wooden stile to reach the road. Turn right, crossing the Nene and passing the old mill. The mill-wheel can still be seen at the right of the building. Across the road is Lower Ringstead Lock where you may be fortunate enough to see a boat passing through. The Nene is said by many to be the loveliest of inland waterways – but if you watch a guillotine lock being operated, you can see that you need to work hard to be able to appreciate it! Continue now along the road, which climbs slightly uphill and then levels out giving fine views up the valley. The Nene winds its way through a series of lakes – even the long Ringstead Island in the middle of the river has its own lake. After about 1/2 mile, just after the road bends to the right, a fishermen's car park is seen on the left.

3. Walk through this car park and down the track to Brightwells Lake. The view up the valley is excellent and you can see the spires of Stanwick and Raunds on the horizon, with Ringstead in the trees to the left. At the bottom of the hill, continue ahead, keeping the lake on your left. A little further around the lake shore, a wooden bridge is seen ahead, and here you leave the lake and cross the bridge on to Ringstead Island. Before the bridge and across the island you can see huge stepping stones, useful here with a river so frequently in flood. This was once a much used path between the villages. Now it is again a popular path - the Nene Way has joined you on your route to Ringstead.

Leave Ringstead Island by way of the high bridge over the navigation channel. To your right is Upper Ringstead Lock, where again you may see the boaters at their labours. The obvious path continues past the sluice and over a little bridge over the mill-tail with its glorious water-lilies. There was once a mill here also – and in medieval times, a village to go with it. The broad track goes past the car parking area and continues to reach a large clearing. This was the site of the old Ringstead and Addington Station – you can see the line of the track to right and left.

4. Continue ahead on the rough track which becomes a tarmacked road, and follow it past the trout and salmon fishery to its end. Now turn left, and after about 50 yards, a squeeze stile on the right will once more lead you to the edge of Kinewell Lake. Bear right around the attractive shore and enjoy the fine views down the water as you return. The lakeside car park is ahead of you on the edge of the village, while for the Axe and Compass you will need to continue a little farther around the lake and then turn away to the right, on the path on which you set out.

PLACES OF INTEREST NEARBY

Just 3 miles away to the north, on opposite banks of the river, are *Thrapston* and *Islip*, both places of interest to transatlantic visitors. Sir John Washington, the great-great-great uncle of the first President, was lord of the manor at Thrapston and lived at Montagu House on Chancery Lane. His coat of arms is on the wall of St James' church in Thrapston, and is said to be the forerunner of the Stars and Stripes. There is a monument to his wife, Lady Mary Washington, in St Nicholas' church in Islip.

ISLIP AND TITCHMARSH NATURE RESERVE

Lying in a wide and fertile valley, the lakes here are all the result of gravel extraction over many years. But now you have a sanctuary where wildfowl and migrating birds share their tranquil abode with butterflies and dragonflies encouraged by the wealth of wild flowers.

Thrapston Lake

Dust ... gravel ... noise ... machinery ... You could never have enjoyed a walk here 30 years ago. But you certainly can today. The gravel extractors have passed on, their legacy a dozen sparkling lakes in a wide green valley. Between and among them flow the Nene and its tributary, Harper's Brook. Man has his recreation here – sailing and fishing are featured in this idyllic setting. But the northern lakes are the preserve of the birds, a breeding ground for golden plover, tern and oyster-catcher and a temporary home and re-fuelling station for thousands of wildfowl and waders on their annual migrations. This is Titchmarsh Local Nature Reserve, and not only are birds drawn to this place, but butterflies of many varieties are attracted by the natural grassland and wild flowers. Dragonflies, too, find the area to their liking, and almost 20 species have been recorded. In the tall trees on the eastern side of the reserve are birds of another kind – herons. The heronry here has been long established and indeed the herons must have survived the incursions of the gravel extractors. In the woodland beneath the nests is an old triangular duck decoy created by one Lord Lilford in 1885. Decoys such as this were used by wealthy gentry to supply birds for their table, but Lord Lilford was President of the British Ornithologists Union, and the birds caught here perhaps suffered only the lesser fate of ringing.

The return route is along the track-bed of the old Northampton-Peterborough Railway, from where through the trees there are many glimpses of Thrapston Lake, the home of the sailing club.

The Rose and Crown is a friendly genuine village local. Built of stone over 300 years ago, inside you can see the old beams and fireplace and low bulging ceiling. The menu is not extensive, but all the essential items are here, the service is prompt and it is very good value. On a fine day, you may appreciate the pleasant garden, where you can enjoy your meal overlooking the valley. Telephone: 01536 733118.

- **HOW TO GET THERE:** From the A14, turn north on the A6116. In about 1/4 mile, at the roundabout, turn right, and then at the bottom of the hill, before the river bridge, turn left into Islip.
- **PARKING:** Street-side parking is possible. There is limited parking at the Rose and Crown for patrons.
- **LENGTH OF THE WALK:** 4 miles. Map: OS Landranger 141 Kettering and Corby (GR 987792).

THE WALK

1. From the corner of the car park of the Rose and Crown, the Nene Way leads down across fields towards the river. When you reach the lane beside the mill, a green fingerpost almost opposite directs you on to a broad grassy track across fields. An attractive stretch along the woodland edge follows and the river sidles in from the right. Soon a footbridge over the river is seen, but you do not cross this. Instead, enter the Nature Reserve, and bear left beside a well-

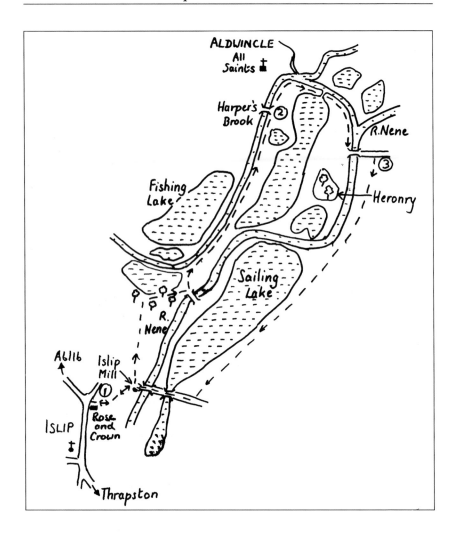

concealed small lake. Gravel extraction in this area produced a remarkable relic – the old Roman bridge which once carried the Gartree Road over the Nene. Nigh on 2,000 years old, its timbers lay well-preserved beneath the river bed. Harper's Brook comes in from the left now, and the way continues beside it, the tower of All Saints church at Aldwincle ahead. Across the brook is a fishing lake, while the large open central lake of the reservation is on your right. This lake and a smaller one are overlooked by hides which you are free to enter – you may wish for your bird book and binoculars here.

Across the lake are the tall trees of the heronry. If the foliage is not too dense you can see the huge nests in the tree tops – the herons add to these each year until they become too heavy and crash to the ground.

2. A pleasant picnic area is reached beside the brook, and here the Nene Way leaves, heading across the bridge. You continue ahead, still beside the brook, and soon the scene opens out to a wide flat meadow with views all around. Here Harper's Brook joins a small branch of the river which has left the main navigation channel. In the distance, churches of the Nene Valley can be seen – to the right, over the lake, the spire of St Nicholas at Islip, and behind you the two churches of Aldwincle, the elegant tower of All Saints now more than matched by the ornate tower at Titchmarsh across the valley. The old grey stone house immediately to the left of All Saints is a former rectory which was the birthplace of the poet John Dryden in 1631. The path curves right and before long you are beside the main river. At the footbridge you leave the reserve and turn left across the river, shortly heading uphill on the broad track.

3. As the track levels out, turn right on to a well-used path with high banks on either side. This is the track-bed of the old railway which you will follow for almost 1½ miles back to Thrapston. At first you are in a deep cutting where you share the path with generations of rabbits enjoying the seclusion. Shortly the banks fall away and glimpses of lakes are to be had through the trees. At the end of the walk, turn right, and, crossing the tip of the lake, head for the bridge in front of Islip Mill. This most picturesque dwelling ceased to be a working mill around 1960. At one time the miller here had a profitable sideline – supplying eels for the London market. From here, you can retrace your steps across the fields to the Rose and Crown.

PLACES OF INTEREST NEARBY

Lyveden New Bield, some 4 miles to the north (off the A6116), is a rather curious building owned by the National Trust. Built by devout Catholic Thomas Tresham around 1600, it is a monument to his faith, being constructed in the form of a cross. It seems also a monument to his interest in mathematics, since ratios of 3, 5, 7 and 9 are everywhere. The booklet will explain it all!

77

THE RIVER NENE AT PICTURESQUE WADENHOE

Is this the finest stretch of the river? Wild flowers in woodland and watermeadow are a treat on this walk, as are the ever-changing views of the spires and towers of the Nene Valley.

Wadenhoe Mill

Wadenhoe is 'a small hillside village apparently made in heaven'. So writes Michael Pearson in his cruising guide to the River Nene and you can certainly see what he means. Warm stone cottages with thatched roofs and roses round the doors tumble down the slopes to the river, while above and apart from them all, a tiny Norman church sits alone on its mysterious hilltop. Wandering through the village you will find Wadenhoe House which was once the home of Sir George Ward-Hunt, a remarkable man who became Chancellor of the Exchequor in Disraeli's government. He installed the country's first rural Telegraph Office here to speed his communications with

London – the old enamel sign still hangs over the post office door. More incredibly, he built his own gasworks to supply lighting to the cottages and streets of the village!

The Nene leaves Wadenhoe passing a picturesque watermill and then wanders on across fields where the spires and towers of tiny distant villages can be seen all around. There are other delights – the lovely woodland path through The Linches, the carved wooden lych-gate and well-head at Achurch and the fine view of the valley from the high ground at Aldwincle. The return path from here to Wadenhoe is very pretty, winding through the trees and offering you little secret glimpses of this loveliest stretch of the river.

Back in Wadenhoe, the King's Head is just what you might expect in an elysian village. An old stone building with tile floors and low beams, its green lawns slope down to the riverside, the perfect setting for an alfresco meal or a drink on a warm summer's evening. The menu changes with the seasons, but there is always an interesting variety of snack lunches and a most exotic choice for the evening with a range of accompanying ales and wines. The Village Hall next door serves excellent cream teas on a Sunday afternoon. Telephone: 01832 720024.

- **HOW TO GET THERE:** Wadenhoe can be reached by turning west off the A605 at Thorpe Waterville north of Thrapston and continuing through Aldwincle.
- **PARKING:** There is a small car park beside the river below the church at Wadenhoe. The King's Head and its car park are right next door to this.
- **LENGTH OF THE WALK:** 6 miles. Map: OS Landranger 141 Kettering and Corby (GR 011834).

THE WALK

1. From the car park beside the river, climb the hill past the King's Head. At the junction, turn down Mill Lane, following the Nene Way signs, and at the bottom continue ahead over the white bridge. As you cross it, glance right to the beautiful old mill, now converted into a private residence. Turn left and follow the path which shortly veers right to a wooden footbridge across the river. The tower and spire which you see on your right are those of the two churches of Aldwincle. The fields you are crossing are part of Wadenhoe Marsh, a Site of Special Scientific Interest. Over the bridge, continue

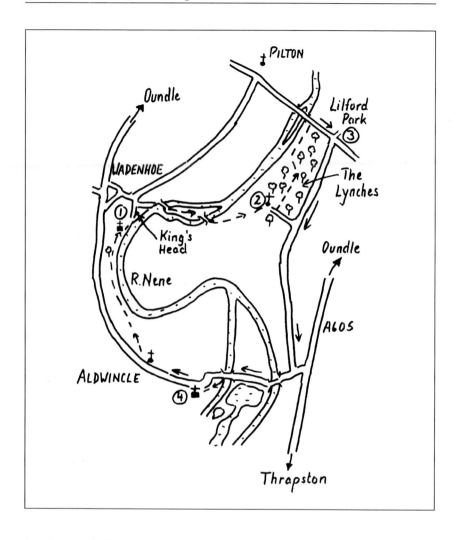

heading uphill towards the spire of St John the Baptist at Achurch. The path runs right through the churchyard and you emerge at the far side through a finely carved oak lych-gate.

2. Continuing ahead, the Nene Way soon turns left on a broad track through The Linches, a beautiful area of mixed woodland. After some distance in the wood, at the track junction, you turn left and take the narrower path which soon goes down some steps. Shortly the river and a lock appear through the trees on your left and the path climbs to reach the road. Turn right and walk on, to reach the gatehouses of 17th-century Lilford Hall.

3. Here turn right (signposted Achurch). The road is long and straight, but there is plenty of interest. In Achurch you pass a huge village well, with an oak canopy similar to the lych-gate you passed through earlier. In 1/2 mile, at Thorpe Waterville, you first keep straight ahead and then at the T-junction turn right on the road to Aldwincle. Two bridges take you across the divided river now, and the raised walkway between them is sometimes the only way to keep your feet dry. This road is often flooded in winter. A footpath on the left will cut off a sharp corner in the road before you reach All Saints church.

4. Continuing up the village street, you have many charming houses to enjoy before reaching the other church, that of St Peter. Just past the church, you again pick up the Nene Way and follow it across a field on the right and between the gardens to reach a large field with fine views where the Nene Way bears left. Ahead of you now are the spires of Achurch and Pilton, and if you are very sharp-eyed – or have brought your binoculars – the slender spire of Oundle can briefly be seen on their left. Behind you is the tower of All Saints, and behind it on the hill, the ornate tower of Titchmarsh. The way takes you on to enter woodland and now the path meanders through the trees with tantalising glimpses of the river through the foliage. At length the stone houses of Wadenhoe appear ahead and you are home. Although the call of the King's Head will be quite strong by this time, resist just a few moments longer. Walk up the hill behind you to the church and look out over the scene where the thatched stone cottages of Wadenhoe peep above the trees on your left and the silvery river below slides silently on its way to the mill.

PLACES OF INTEREST NEARBY

More of the great outdoors is on offer at *Barnwell Country Park*, on the A605, 1/2 mile south of Oundle. In an area of lakes beside the river, you will find picnic places, woodland paths, nature trails, a huge variety of waterfowl and an award-winning visitor centre. Telephone: 01832 273435.

WALK 18

THE RIVER NENE BETWEEN OUNDLE AND ASHTON

The Nene describes a huge curve around the lovely old market town of Oundle. Colourful narrow boats, peacocks on the village green and the exquisite spire of Oundle parish church all contribute to this most enjoyable walk.

A branch of the Nene near Oundle

The River Nene seems to reject Oundle town and turning away, prefers instead a long journey through the water meadows to the east. This is the scene of your walk, a wide flat green valley where cattle browse, wildfowl graze and herons stand in silence beside the tranquil water. In the lazy heat of a summer's day, huge yellow water-lilies drift in the shallows and dragonflies on filmy wings hover over the banks. A peaceful scene it is, and dragonflies are so much attracted to this place that the riverside mill here has been converted into the National Dragonfly Museum – a fascinating place to visit. But this is for the end of the walk. First comes a stroll beside the looping river, completing the circle with a contrasting walk through Oundle town. Mellow stone houses, antiques shops, tea rooms and school buildings are jumbled together around the old square and all are watched over by the 200 foot crocketted spire of St Peter's church.

The walk ends – and starts – at the unique little village of Ashton, where matching thatched cottages ring a village green shaded by horse chestnut trees and the scene is rounded off with a pub in the same style. Ashton's story is that it was rebuilt around 1900 by Charles Rothschild from nearby Ashton Wold, who planned here a model village for his workforce. He adapted Ashton Mill on the river (now the National Dragonfly Museum) to provide water and electricity for the cottages and included in each something very extravagant for 1900 – a bathroom! Charles Rothschild was a man of many parts and among his interests were lepidoptera. The pub was named after a favourite butterfly, the Chequered Skipper, which now, alas, is extinct. The pub, too, almost became extinct in 1996, when a fire, starting in the thatch, soon razed it to the ground. Happily, it was rebuilt and is here today to provide welcome refreshment after your journey.

The glory of the Chequered Skipper is its setting – its 'beer garden' is the village green! Peacocks from Ashton Wold wander freely here, and in summer eating outdoors is popular with frequent barbecues. But there are tables inside too, and meals are served here every lunchtime and evening. The menu – chalked on the board – offers some mouth-watering selections and 'different' dishes – among them emu steaks and venison. As a freehouse, a wide range of beers, and particularly local brews, are on offer to accompany the meal.

Telephone: 01832 273494.

- **HOW TO GET THERE:** At the roundabout on the A605 just north of Oundle, turn right (signposted to Polebrook). In about 1/2 mile, turn left where signposted to reach the village of Ashton.
- **PARKING:** Walkers may leave their cars around the green or in the limited parking area beside the Chequered Skipper.
- **LENGTH OF THE WALK:** 3½ miles. Maps: OS Landranger 141 Kettering and Corby, and OS Landranger 142 Peterborough (GR 056883).

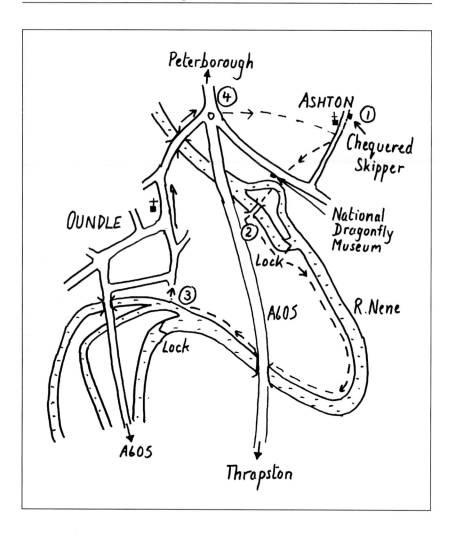

1. Walk away from the Chequered Skipper across the village green beneath the horse chestnut trees. Herein lies Ashton's other claim to fame - on one Sunday each October it hosts the World Conker Championships. This may sound a bit grand, but indeed players come from very distant parts and the game is taken most seriously, even if the surrounding stalls and festivities give the day a more carnival-like atmosphere. Below the green, keep beside the churchyard wall following the Nene Way signs and pass through the gate into a field where sheep usually graze.

The elegant spire of St Peter's church at Oundle is ahead of you and it will keep you company throughout your walk. At the bottom of the field, cross the road and turn right for about 50 yards to reach the buildings of Ashton Mill, now the National Dragonfly Museum. Turn left here, and through the buildings, take the track which leads on to a metal bridge over the river.

2. Over the bridge, turn left and keep to the river bank. Water rushes over the weirs on your left, while Ashton Lock hides itself behind the trees. The path is well marked as you cross the field beside the lock and then return to the water's edge. This is a truly lovely stretch, and particularly so on a summer's day when the heat seems to settle in these water meadows. The river is popular with boaters and the bright colours of narrow boats and sparkling whites of cruisers complement the scene. The curving river guides you around and soon you are again heading for that spire. The path passes under the old railway bridge which now carries the Oundle bypass, and continues through a wooded stretch to reach a lovely meadow dotted with pollarded willows. The gates of Lower Barnwell Lock appear on the left and at the little metal footbridge you must turn away and leave the river.

3. Cross the field on your right to a wooden gate. Walk uphill on the road and at its end, turn right and continue past the end of Herne Road into St Osyth's Lane. This will lead you on to the Market Place. Here you must surely pause a while and take in the scene. At the centre is the old Town Hall, built in the 19th century of stone from an old church at Barnwell, opposite is Oundle School Bookshop with its colonnade, and to your right and along North Street (where you will be going in a minute) are some of Oundle's oldest houses, many now part of Oundle School. Opposite, across North Street, the steps lead up to the church, and to the left of them is Laxton School with its cloisters. Laxton is the non-boarding part of Oundle School and is named after Sir William Laxton, a 16th century Lord Mayor of London, who originally came from this town. Continuing now along North Street, you eventually come out by a playing field and then cross the river on North Bridge. Oundle was once the head of navigation, and on the west side of the bridge is the old Oundle Wharf. On the other side, the old station buildings are passed as you continue to the roundabout.

Picnic tables on the green at the Chequered Skipper

4. Cross the A605 (with care!) to a footpath fingerpost on the bank opposite. This leads you uphill with the hedge on your left. Soon you wind through a little woodland and emerge again with the hedge on the same side. The whole area is very popular with rabbits – beware tripping on their burrows! A stile leads on into a field where you keep to the left-hand side beside a wood. At the stone wall, cross over the stile and pass the chapel, to arrive again at Ashton village green and its Chequered Skipper.

PLACES OF INTEREST NEARBY

The *National Dragonfly Museum* which you pass near the start of your walk is quite unique. You could never imagine such a wealth of information on the modest dragonfly, and all most attractively presented with indoor exhibits, outdoor trails, and even a tea room. It is open only on summer weekends from June to September, but it may be worth timing your walk accordingly. Telephone: 01832 272427.

THE NENE BELOW NASSINGTON

Here the river is calm and peaceful, wandering through wide water meadows before it glides silently under Wansford Bridge and is gone – at least from Northamptonshire! Picturesque villages of warm local stone contribute to make this a most memorable walk.

Wansford Bridge

On this walk you are following the river on the final stages of its journey through its native county. In this wide and shallow valley there is much evidence of previous Roman occupation. Two miles away to the east the large fort of Durobrivae was built where the London to York road, Ermine Street, crossed the Nene. The Romans were the first to quarry the stone in this area – an activity which has continued over the centuries since. The stone is lovely – a warm honey-coloured ironstone, which makes the villages in these parts most attractive.

At Nassington where you begin, the old stone houses are topped by Collyweston slates and are complemented by the lovely crocketted spire of St Mary and All Saints church, while the 13th-century Prebendal Manor House is the oldest continuously inhabited house in the county (telephone 01780 782575 for details of when it is open to the public). Yarwell was a centre for stonemasons in the 18th and 19th centuries and is known for its fine houses. At Wansford an elegant old bridge spans the wide river and on its far bank is an interesting row of honey-stone buildings, among them the famous old Haycock Hotel, a former coaching inn on the Great North Road. The return route is similarly pleasing. At first the way leads through the Old Sulehay Forest, which was once the site of a Roman stone quarry. Beyond the forest, you walk through the site of a much more recent quarry which has been made a Nature Conservation area. The way home leads over a hill with distant views before a gentle descent across farmland guided by the spire of Nassington church.

In a village of old properties, the Black Horse itself dates from 1674, although quite a lot of alteration has gone on since. It is a listed building with some interesting features inside, most notably a fireplace from Fotheringhay Castle, and a bar made from old doors from Rufford Abbey. The menu is suitably impressive, too! Expect to spend quite some time regarding those blackboards with their chalked-up 'specials'. The Black Horse is well known for its cuisine and from time to time organises evenings of gourmet feasting, accompanied by music. But if your requirements are rather more humble, you will also find an excellent snack menu, and, of course, a suitably wide range of ales to accompany it.

Telephone: 01780 782324.

- **HOW TO GET THERE:** From the A605, 2 miles north of Oundle, turn where signposted to Fotheringhay. In the village, turn right opposite the church and continue through to Nassington.
- **PARKING:** On quiet roads in the village. There is parking for patrons at the Black Horse which is on the road from Fotheringhay as you enter the village.
- **LENGTH OF THE WALK:** 5 miles. Map: OS Landranger 142 Peterborough (GR 067963).

THE WALK

1. From the Black Horse, turn right on Station Road, and take the footpath on the left just after the end house. You are now on the

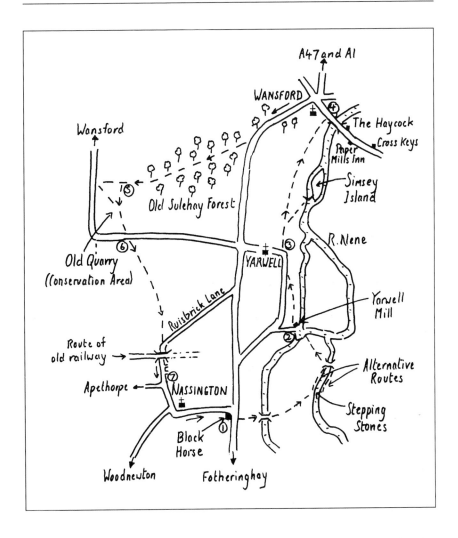

Nene Way which is well signposted and you will have no difficulty following it through to Yarwell Mill. After crossing the main river, the old route of the Nene Way took you across a lesser branch on stepping stones, which are still in place. You can go that way if you fancy the adventure!

2. Arriving at the mill with its attractive caravan site, cross the lock and continue on the road beside the water and moored boats. Just past the red and white entrance barrier, a Nene Way sign directs you to turn right along the edge of a field. At the sign with two yellow footprints, bear left and continue across the field diagonally to reach the road on the far side. Here turn right and walk into the village of Yarwell. There are some lovely old stone buildings on the right, and on the corner, the old Yarwell Manor.

3. Where the road swings left, you continue ahead on the path following the direction signs. Soon you enter a field where there are wide views over the river valley and you can see a lock on this side of Simsey Island, which is the largest island in the Nene. It is possible to visit it, following the signs. Returning again, it is easy to follow the Nene Way across the fields towards Wansford. From the final field there is a lovely view of the ancient bridge, where boats are moored beside the water meadows.

4. Emerging at a stile beside the bridge, it is well worth crossing the river to look at the Haycock Hotel on the other bank. The story behind its name is a well known one which you can guess from the sign. A local farm-worker, no doubt made drowsy by ale, fell asleep on a haycock one hot summer's afternoon. A thunderstorm broke, the river rose, and the haycock was carried downstream. The lad was wakened by the shouts of spectators on the bank, and enquired of them where he had reached. On being told 'Wansford', he replied, 'What, Wansford in England?' – and the place has been called Wansford-in-England ever since.

There are two more inns offering refreshment along this road. To continue with the walk, return over the bridge and keep ahead to where the church stands on the corner. Here turn left down the Yarwell Road and follow it down and then uphill through woodland. Shortly after leaving the woodland, turn right on a bridleway which leads you directly into Old Sulehay Forest. Now dense trees crowd beside your path and in the undergrowth wild flowers thrive in the deep shade – wood anemones, woodruff and the early purple orchid among others. Leaving the wood, a deep quarry, usually with some water at the bottom, is seen on the left. Soon after this, look for a gap in the hedge on the left where you enter the quarry.

5. The one-time stone quarry is now a conservation area where some splendid regeneration has taken place. Humps and hollows are colonised by clumps of silver birch, the dog rose thrives, traveller's joy hangs from the many low shrubs and wild flowers of unusual kinds flourish on the sandy earth. On entering the quarry, you should take the left hand of the three paths in front of you. This path soon sweeps around and passes through silver birch to reach a clearing. Here, bear left, again through a spinney of silver birch to reach a second clearing, where you see a sign board ahead of you. Opposite the sign board, on the left, is a stile, and crossing this takes you along a grassy path to reach the road.

6. Cross straight over the road to the stile opposite. Cross the first small field directly, and then cut across the corner of the second field to a gap in the left-hand hedge, beneath a large oak tree. Now bear diagonally left uphill across this field. From the top of the ridge, the spire of Nassington can be seen ahead, and heading towards this, you pass through a gap in the next hedge. As you continue in the direction of the spire, your path through the grassy fields becomes more obvious. At the bottom of the last field, bear left and pass through a gate into Ruisbrick Lane. Here you turn right, and continue under the railway bridge to reach the edge of Nassington, where you keep straight ahead to the main road.

7. Here, turn left into the village, where there is plenty of interest. The church is usually open and you will find, among other things, the shaft of a Saxon cross in the north aisle. Opposite the church is the Prebendal Manor, which was built around 1230. Past the church, the lovely old stone houses continue, and you can savour them all the way to the end of the road and the Black Horse.

PLACES OF INTEREST NEARBY
Wansford is the western terminus of the *Nene Valley Railway*, which runs alongside the river for 7 miles to Peterborough. The station is situated off the A1, just south of the village. The trains, which are mostly steam, run every weekend from February to November, and more frequently during the school holidays. Telephone: 01780 784444.

WILLOW BROOK AND BLATHERWYCKE LAKE

Through the heart of the ancient Rockingham Forest winds Willow Brook, and here you follow its course through a gentle valley and along the tree-lined shores of Blatherwycke Lake. Returning through the forest itself, you may be lucky enough to meet deer.

Beside Blatherwycke Lake

Willow Brook must breathe a sigh of relief as it leaves its birthplace amid the industry of Corby and hurries out on the loveliest of courses into the depths of Rockingham Forest. Three times it is held back on its journey to the Nene, each time to provide an ornamental lake in the grounds of a country house. Following its rushing waters upstream from King's Cliffe, you come upon the largest of these lakes at Blatherwycke and can marvel that a lake of such size was ever created by human hand. In this case the hands were those of Irish labourers, glad to escape their country in the days of the potato famine, and the masters for whom they worked were the Stafford family of Blatherwycke Hall.

There is no Blatherwycke Hall to be seen today – it was demolished at the end of the Second World War during which it had been a base for troops. But besides the lake there are other reminders of its greatness – the tiny church with its memorials, the grand pillars at the old gates, the knot emblems on the walls of the houses and parapets of the bridge and, most curiously, the lonely statue of a Greek Archer who has exchanged his formal garden setting for that of a common cornfield. From the bridge in the little stone village of Blatherwycke you can enjoy a most attractive view of the reedy tree-shaded lake and all its wildfowl. Farther on up the hill, you come upon the handsome stone buildings of Fineshade Abbey – or rather the stables of the Georgian mansion which was built on its site. The deep forest then waits for you, and you will be grateful that the narrow path through it is so well marked. The kings who hunted here are long since gone, but the deer are still in residence and your silence could well be rewarded by a sighting of these beautiful creatures.

King's Cliffe was once the chief town of one of the three 'bailiwicks' of the forest, and the home of a royal hunting lodge. Much quieter today, there is still much to admire, not least the fine old stone houses of West Street as you return towards the church. Among them is the Cross Keys inn, itself an 18th-century building of local stone, and the sole survivor of several pubs in the village. It is a freehouse, and you can enjoy a variety of ales. Meals are very reasonable, wholesome and well served, extending from sandwiches to a range of steaks in various guises. 'Puddings' (not desserts!) – hot chocolate fudge cake with rich cream, steamed roly-poly, etc., – appear ideal for hearty appetites induced by walking!

Telephone: 01780 470276.

- **HOW TO GET THERE:** King's Cliffe lies just east of the A43 Kettering-Stamford road and can be reached from that road by turning where signed.
- **PARKING:** On quiet roadsides in the village near the church. There is also parking for patrons at the Cross Keys.
- **LENGTH OF THE WALK:** 7½ miles. Map: OS Landranger 141 Kettering and Corby (GR 006971).

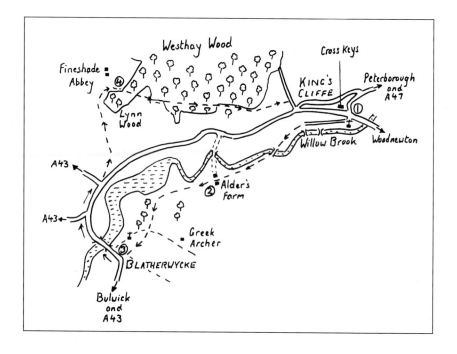

THE WALK

1. From the Cross Keys, cross the road to the church and turn down Church Walk. Running between high walls and interesting houses, this emerges at a green on the left where you continue ahead. Soon a track crosses your way, and again you continue ahead over a waymarked stile, past allotments and along the side of a field. Cross a second field keeping the hedge on your right, and in the third field bear left downhill to cross Willow Brook on a wooden bridge. Now turn right and fcllow the rushing brook along its attractive wooded banks. After four fields, you reach Alders Farm and pass between the barns and the houses.

2. Keeping the same direction, continue ahead across the field where the path should be clear. The brook is below you to the right. Soon you reach a hedge on your left at the top of the field. Following along it, there is a gap in the hedge and you should go through this and continue in the same direction (you really have no choice, as ahead is marked No Right of Way!). A sign on the gate tells you to keep to the waymarked path – but of course there is not a waymark in sight. Nevertheless, the hedge on your right soon gives way to woodland, and glimpses of Blatherwycke Lake appear through the trees. You are in a lovely sweeping valley here, its rims crowned by tracts of forest. Without a habitation in sight, this peaceful place feels quite remote – far-away enough for the occasional sighting of red kite. Suddenly the trees clear and for the first time you can see across this sizeable lake. How long did it take to dig this by hand? It seems odd that this rural lake has more recently been used to supply water to the steel works of Corby. Walking on past woods full of pheasant and partridge, you climb above the lake and descend again on a stony track. Looking to the left on this descent, you can see the statue known as the Greek Archer all alone in a field – no doubt he once had pride of place in the gardens of Blatherwycke Hall. After continuing straight ahead at the cross-tracks, you reach the road at a sharp corner.

3. On the cottages ahead of you, the emblem of the lovers knot can be seen. The initials S.O.B. and the knot refer to the joining in marriage of the Stafford and O'Brien families. Turn right on the road and follow it past the old entrance gates to the stone bridge in the village – where once again, that knot is in evidence. This end of the lake is delightful, truly a picture postcard scene. Silent herons conceal themselves in banks of reeds and bulrushes while the waters abound with wildfowl going about their business. When you are ready to go on, continue on the road to the second junction. Here take the footpath between the two roads and climb gently uphill on the well-marked path. At a gap in the hedge at the top of the hill, bear left downhill across the field to the lowest edge of the woodland. Fineshade Abbey comes into view as you go. Follow the woodland edge around to descend to the stream, cross the sheep compound and then bear right uphill again to reach a corner of woodland near the top.

4. Here there is a green metal gate, and on the other side of it, a broad track into the wood. Following this you will be pleased to come upon a waymark at last. The track swings right, but the waymark directs you ahead on a narrow path through the wood. The route is now superbly waymarked, and emerging on the far side, you cut across a field corner and again follow outside the woodland edge. At the corner of a field the waymarks direct you

The Greek Archer spotted on the walk

once more into the wood on your left. Following the waymarks for some distance, you come upon the track bed of an old railway, and eventually arrive at a stile into a field. Now keep ahead with the wood on your left, and the trees lining the railway cutting away on your right. As you continue across the fields, the railway cutting approaches your path and you are soon walking beside it. Reaching a broad stony track, turn right to cross the railway and go ahead to the road junction. Here turn left down West Street to return to the church and the Cross Keys.

PLACES OF INTEREST NEARBY

If you fancy more woodland trails, there are plenty to be had. The Forestry Commission's Headquarters are at *Top Lodge*, just off the A43, 3 miles from King's Cliffe. Here there are forest routes marked with coloured posts. Off the A43 opposite is *Wakerley Great Wood* with footpaths and permanent orienteering routes (obtainable from Top Lodge).

Deene Park is a lovely Tudor and Georgian mansion off the A43, 4 miles south of King's Cliffe. Here again is an ornamental lake created from Willow Brook, amid fine landscaped gardens. Open summer Sundays and Bank Holidays. Telephone: 01780 450278.